Pass the Highway Code Test

Brenda Ralph Lewis

foulsham
LONDON • NEW YORK • TORONTO • SYDNEY

foulsham
The Publishing House, Bennetts Close
Cippenham, Berkshire, SL1 5AP, England.

While every effort has been made to ensure the accuracy of all the information contained within this book, neither the author nor the publisher can be liable for any errors. In particular, since laws change from time to time, it is vital that each individual should check relevant legal details for themselves.

ISBN 0-572-02283-2

Copyright © 1996 W. Foulsham & Co. Ltd.

All rights reserved.
The Copyright Act (1956) prohibits (subject to certain very limited exceptions) the making of copies of any copyright work or of a substantial part of such a work, including the making of copies by photocopying or similar process.
Written permission to make a copy or copies must therefore normally be obtained from the publisher in advance. It is advisable also to consult the publisher if in any doubt as to the legality of any copying which is to be undertaken.

Phototypeset in Great Britain by Typesetting Solutions, Slough, Berks.
Printed in Great Britain by Cox & Wyman Ltd, Reading, Berks.

CONTENTS

	Page
Introduction	4
1. The Road	5
2. Other Road Users	10
3. Driving Conditions and Night Driving	17
4. Motorways, Primary Routes and Local Roads	23
5. You and Your Car	30
6. Markings on the Road	33
7. Signs on the Road	37
8. Roundabouts and Level Crossings	43
9. Parking and Waiting	47
10. Breakdowns, Accidents and Mishaps	52
11. First Aid on the Road	55
12. Road Junctions and Traffic Lights	58
13. Three Driver's Tales	61
14. Traffic Signs	65
15. The Theory Test	72
Answers	77
Index	126

INTRODUCTION

This book is designed to help you acquire a sound knowledge of the Highway Code in an enjoyable and straightforward way. The subjects covered in the Code have been divided with separate sections concentrating, for example, on 'The Road', 'You and Your Car', 'Road Signs' and so on. In this way, you can get a close insight into each major factor that makes up the Code and also into 'reading the road' while driving. You can also clear each aspect in your mind before moving on.

Naturally, there are cross-over points between sections and you will find different aspects of a topic treated in more than one place; repetition itself being an aid to learning. Afterwards you can select questions at random to test your understanding. The index can help to locate questions on specific topics.

All this aims, firstly, to acquaint you with matters of law relating to the use of the road. Secondly, it aims to concentrate your attention on the business of driving, using your own common sense and awareness of safety and consideration for others. Finally, it aims to teach you the language of the road: the meaning of its signs, signals and markings. As well as being the aims of this book, these are the basic purposes of the Highway Code. And since, from mid 1996, these skills are being tested with a multiple-choice theory test, we have included a sample test so that you can try out the format which you will be expected to follow when you take the theory part of your driving test.

Section One
The Road

1. How close to the car in front of you may you drive, as a general rule of safety on the road?

2. You are driving along the road at a safe cruising speed when a vehicle overtakes you and moves into the gap between your car and the car in front. What should you do?

3. When driving along a fogbound road, what is your stopping distance?

4. On a dry road, in good driving conditions, what is the minimum stopping distance for a car going at the following speeds?
   a) 60 mph.
   b) 40 mph.
   c) 30 mph.

5. In the Highway Code, shortest or minimum stopping distances comprise THINKING and BRAKING distances added together. What is the THINKING DISTANCE for a motorist who has to stop when driving at the following speeds?
   a) 70 mph.
   b) 50 mph.
   c) 30 mph.

PASS YOUR HIGHWAY CODE TEST

6. What is the BRAKING DISTANCE for a car going at 40 mph?

7. When driving at 20 mph, the shortest stopping distance is 40 feet (12 m). How is this divided between THINKING and BRAKING distances?

8. When a bus in front indicates that it is about to move out from a bus stop, what should you do?

9. What is the first and most important requirement a motorist must observe when driving in fog?

10. Can you name two particular disadvantages from which cyclists suffer when on the road?

11. What can you do to prevent yourself from becoming sleepy when driving on a long journey or when driving on the motorway?

12. At what speed in mph is the BRAKING DISTANCE twice the THINKING DISTANCE?

13. In fog, what should you do if a vehicle comes up close behind you; close enough, let us say, to 'fill' your rear-view mirror?

14. In wet and slippery road conditions, how can you quickly and easily reckon the appropriate gap between your car and the car in front of you?

THE ROAD

15. In Britain you normally drive on the left of the road. However, you are sometimes permitted to move to the right. Can you name at least three situations in which you can do this?

16. There are stationary vehicles and some pedestrians at the side of a road along which you are driving. What should you do when you drive past them?

17. Name three people who are authorised to direct or signal instructions to cars on the road.

18. When carrying loads, what three rules must you follow?

19. A lane control signal over a road has four small box panels, two of which show green downward pointing arrows. Two of the box panels show red 'X's. How many lanes are open on this road?

20. A green direction sign indicates a roundabout from which roads are shown leading to four destinations. How many exits/entrances are there on this roundabout?

21. What does 'R' printed on a green, yellow-edged road sign mean?

22. On the road surface, how are traffic lane directions indicated by markings?

PASS YOUR HIGHWAY CODE TEST

23. You see a long, horizontal, black sign with white chevrons pointing to the right. What does this tell you about the road ahead?

24. You are approaching a set of traffic lights. What is indicated if they show the following?
    a) An amber light on its own.
    b) Red and amber lights together.
    c) A red light with a green filter arrow pointing left.

25. You are not allowed to stop on a motorway except when your car breaks down and you can't help it, or in an emergency such as stopping in order to prevent an accident. Name three other circumstances in which you can stop on a motorway.

26. What is the deceleration lane on a motorway?

27. You are driving along a motorway when you see that the overhead panel above your lane is showing a lighted arrow. This indicates a turn to the left. What does this mean?

28. Special signs on motorways advise you of road conditions ahead. How do these signs tell you that normal conditions prevail?

29. There is a flashing amber signal on the motorway. What is it telling you?

THE ROAD

30. You are driving along a motorway, heading for your holiday destination. Your family's luggage is stowed on the roof of your car when suddenly a suitcase falls off and lands on the road. You should stop immediately and go back to retrieve it. *TRUE* or *FALSE*?

31. When you are driving along a road, in what circumstances are you permitted to switch on your hazard warning lights?

32. Your car has broken down on the road. To warn other drivers, at what distance should you place your reflecting red triangle warning sign ...
    a) On an ordinary road (for instance, an A or B road)?
    b) On a motorway?

33. People on motorcycles must wear properly fastened safety helmets and must sit on a proper seat with their feet on foot rests. What else should they do (four things)?

34. What MUST a learner motorcyclist do before going on the road?

35. The Highway Code says you must obey traffic light signals and what else?

36. What four things should you do before moving off?

PASS YOUR HIGHWAY CODE TEST

37. Unless signs show otherwise, what is the speed limit in a road with street lights?

38. In some areas the speed limit may be lower than 30 mph. What is it likely to be?

39. Sometimes it is not safe to drive at the speed limit. What four specific conditions, when you should slow down, does the Highway Code list?

40. Before you reverse, what should you check for and what should you be aware of?

Section Two
Other Road Users

41. According to the Highway Code, what is the definition of a Heavy Goods Vehicle?

42. Describe the markings carried at the back of Heavy Goods Vehicles to warn other road users of their presence.

43. What hand signal do you use when you wish to inform drivers behind you that you are about to turn left or move left?

44. At Zebra crossings, how do you let pedestrians know you are about to stop for them?

OTHER ROAD USERS

45. Broken, thick white lines are painted across carriageways to indicate those places where you must give way to other traffic. Whereabouts do the following markings appear?
    a) Small, box-like, white rectangles painted close together.
    b) Two parallel lines of longer white rectangles painted fairly close together.
    c) A single line of longer white rectangles spaced their own width apart on the road.

46. Which white, black-edged, rectangular sign indicates a bus lane on the road at the junction ahead?

47. A sign indicating a parking place for caravans shows a caravan in silhouette and one other feature. What is it?

48. Which sign indicates a route that is recommended for pedal cyclists?

49. When should you look into your rear-view mirrors while driving.

50. The road conditions are good. The road is dry and the sun is shining, but fortunately not into your eyes. How should you make a quick reckoning of the proper gap between your car and the car in front of you?

51. Name three types of emergency vehicle for which you should always make way on the road.

PASS YOUR HIGHWAY CODE TEST

52. Which of the following is permitted to drive in the *RIGHT HAND LANE* of a motorway carriageway with three or more lanes?
    a) A bus or coach 9 metres long.
    b) A bus or coach over 12 metres long.
    c) A vehicle towing a trailer.
    d) A goods vehicle with operating weight of 5 tonnes.
    e) A vehicle with operating weight of more than 7½ tonnes.

53. You have overtaken a car on the motorway. What should your next move be?

54. What does it mean if you see a vehicle flashing blue lights or hear one sounding sirens?

55. You are driving along a road in fairly heavy traffic. Some distance in front, on the left-hand side of your lane, you see two people riding horses. Each rider has only one hand on the bridle of their own horse. With the other, they are holding the bridles of horses which they are leading. As you drive past the two riders, which horses — those being ridden or those being led — should be nearer to you?

56. Where should motorists be particularly watchful for animals and how should they drive past them?

57. Which of the following are permitted to use motorways?
    a) Combine harvesters.

OTHER ROAD USERS

   b) Learner drivers.
   c) Pedal cyclists.
   d) Motorcycles over 50 cc.
   e) Pedestrians.

58. You notice a hitchhiker on the slip road at the approach to a motorway and want to give him a lift. Can you?

59. You are driving along a road with a gentle bend to the left ahead. It is after sunset and you can't see the other road users, who are just rounding the bend, very clearly. However, you *can* see a white light being carried in front and a red light also being carried a little way behind. So who or what is using the road at that point?

60. You have reached your destination and have parked by the side of the road in the correct position. You move to open your car door to get out, but what must you do first?

61. Particularly when driving at night, you should always take care that your headlights do not dazzle other drivers. It is not, however, just a matter of dipping your headlights when other drivers are around. In which of the following situations should you dip your headlamps?
   a) When driving on a lighted motorway or other high speed road.
   b) When driving along a well-lit road in a built-up area.
   c) When the light from your headlamps can reach the driver of the vehicle in front of you.

PASS YOUR HIGHWAY CODE TEST

d) When another vehicle approaches from the opposite direction.

62. In what circumstances are you permitted to flash your headlamps?

63. In what circumstances can you sound the horn on your car?

64. A vehicle is approaching from the right and is signalling with its left-hand indicator. Should you drive on past it?

65. As a general rule, on which side of the vehicle in front should you overtake?

66. What must you watch out for when entering or driving out of a property which borders on a road?

67. When MUST you stop at a Zebra crossing?

68. Pedestrians are standing by the side of the road, waiting to cross. You intend to slow down and let them traverse the road but should not signal to them to do so. Why?

69. You come upon white zigzag lines on either side of the driving lane, marked in the road. What lies ahead? What do the zigzags mean?

70. When a queue of traffic crosses a pedestrian crossing what must you do?

OTHER ROAD USERS

71. When a Pelican pedestrian crossing has a central refuge, does this count as two separate crossings?

72. What is written on the sign used by School Crossing Patrols?

73. You are first on the scene of an accident. What information should you particularly note in order to give the details to the emergency services?

74. When approaching a level crossing, do you stop *ONLY* when the red STOP signs light up?

75. You see the letters HR on a local direction sign (a rectangular panel with yellow background and black lettering). Who would you expect to find using the road with this sign?

76. Diamond-shaped information panels are carried by vehicles containing dangerous goods or substances. The panels include wording and a picture symbol in each case, *viz.,* TOXIC, with a skull and crossbones depicted above it, on a plain white diamond. What picture symbol and background colour is used to denote each of the following?
a) Toxic.
b) Spontaneously combustible.
c) Compressed gas.
d) Radioactive.
e) Corrosive.
f) Oxidising agent.
g) Flammable liquid.

PASS YOUR HIGHWAY CODE TEST

77. When the load on a vehicle overhangs the front or the rear of the vehicle by more than 2 metres, an additional projection marker must be carried. Describe this projection marker.

78. What should you do about signals given by other road users (two things)?

79. What is the only time you are allowed to drive over a pavement?

80. What kind of warning lights do slow-moving vehicles carry?

81. Of course, horses are animals so you must be careful near them, but the Highway Code gives another reason for special care. What is it?

82. Can you drive in a cycle lane marked with ...
    a) A broken white line?
    b) A solid white line?

83. What six things should you do if you want to overtake?

84. What two things should you do once you have started overtaking someone?

85. How much room should you give motorcyclists, cyclists or horse riders when passing them?

86. In which two situations can you overtake on the left?

OTHER ROAD USERS

87. How should you drive when being overtaken?

88. You must not overtake after a 'No Overtaking' sign, or in the zigzag area of a pedestrian crossing, or where there are double lines in the road with a solid one near you. Name 12 other places where you should not overtake.

Section Three
Driving Conditions and Night Driving

89. A red-edged, white, triangular sign warns of a ford in the road ahead. What does the sign show?

90. Are you allowed to let your vehicle wait in the following places?
    a) In the area of zigzag lines on either side of a Zebra crossing.
    b) On the right-hand side of a one-way street at night.
    c) In the area indicated by zigzag lines on the approach to a Pelican crossing.
    d) On the left-hand side of the road at night.
    e) In a bus lane.
    f) On a road marked with double white lines.

91. In a built-up area, when must you not sound your car horn?

PASS YOUR HIGHWAY CODE TEST

92. On a dry road, in good conditions, you suddenly have to stop and you do so in the minimum stopping distance of 240 feet (73 m). What was your speed?

93. Where road conditions are wet, should the minimum stopping distance for your car relative to its speed be: at least trebled, or at least doubled or at least quadrupled?

94. When may vehicles other than buses use a specially designated bus lane?

95. When overtaking, what special difficulties must you bear in mind when conditions are foggy or misty, or when it is dusk or night-time?

96. You find yourself in a traffic queue and want to move into another lane on the left in order to overtake. Is it permitted to do this?

97. You are about to turn into a road at a junction. What should you particularly look out for on the road into which you are turning?

98. On a motorway, how do the special signs which give information about road conditions show that conditions are normal?

99. On some motorways, amber signals may be used to denote slippery roads ahead or foggy conditions. Describe how the signals operate.

DRIVING CONDITIONS

100. You see a long, horizontal, black sign ahead with white chevrons pointing to the left. What does this tell you?

101. You see a sign (a white, red-edged triangle) showing an exclamation mark in black. What does it mean?

102. Describe the overhead motorway sign which means *DO NOT MOVE FURTHER ALONG THIS LANE*.

103. You are ON a level crossing when, suddenly, you realise that the amber warning lights on the automatic half-barrier are showing and you can hear the alarm. From these signals, you know a train is approaching. What should you do?

104. You wish to turn right from a side road into a dual carriageway, but the central reservation is too narrow for your vehicle to pause there safely. What should you do?

105. You come upon a herd of animals being led along the road. What should you particularly avoid doing in these circumstances?

106. What is the significance of a single broken line, with long markings and short gaps, in the middle of the road?

107. If you are driving a large or slow-moving vehicle and wish to pass over a level crossing, how do you ensure it is safe to do so?

108. At an 'open' level crossing, how can you make sure that there are no trains approaching?

109. In an area where you are permitted to park your vehicle at night without lights, what is the minimum distance you should park it from a road junction?

110. If your car breaks down at night, why is it inadvisable to stand at the rear of the vehicle?

111. Automatic level crossings have amber lights followed by flashing red STOP lights. If a train passes over the crossing but the lights continue to flash, what does this mean?

112. Where a vehicle is permitted to park at night without lights, should you place it facing in, or opposing, the direction of traffic flow on the road?

113. Suppose you come upon an accident involving a vehicle carrying dangerous goods — what additional information (apart from the fact of the accident) should you report to the emergency services?

114. What is the significance of a pedestrian carrying a white stick with two red, reflectorised bands?

DRIVING CONDITIONS

115. Children and elderly pedestrians may share a potentially dangerous characteristic. What is it?

116. When an information sign shows a short, horizontal, *RED* bar across a line indicating a route, what does this mean?

117. Why should vehicles not wait or park on the brow of a hill or at a hump-backed bridge?

118. When must you use your headlamps, not just your sidelights, while driving at night?
    a) On roads with no street lighting.
    b) Where the street lamps are not alight.
    c) Where street lamps are 200 metres apart.
    d) Where visibility is reduced — perhaps by fog — to less than 200 metres.

119. Tinted spectacles, worn while driving can help cut out sunshine glare, but should you wear them at night?

120. Two triangular, red-edged, white signs warn of the road narrowing ahead. Both comprise two parallel lines, but in one the right-hand line has an inward kink. In the other, both lines kink towards each other. What do each of these signs indicate?

121. What road sign indicates the presence of wild animals in the vicinity?

122. List 11 things you should do in fog.

PASS YOUR HIGHWAY CODE TEST

123. What two things should you do to get your car ready for winter?

124. You should be careful in freezing conditions. What situation does the Highway Code particularly mention?

125. If you have to drive in snow you should go slowly, steering and changing speed gently. What should you also do to avoid wheel spin.

126. When can you overtake a snow-plough?

127. At road works you should get into lane early, watch for vehicles leaving the works area, and not overtake traffic waiting in a queue. But what else?

Section Four
Motorways, Primary Routes and Local Roads

Motorways

128. What sign is used to indicate the start of a motorway?

129. What is the most noticeable difference between signs on motorways and those on other roads, such as primary or local roads?

130. What four things should you remember concerning your speed on the motorway?

131. A motorway sign shows 'M10 (M1)'. What does this signify?

132. *TRUE* or *FALSE*: on the motorway, you are allowed to overtake ...
   a) In a lane on the left.
   b) On the hard shoulder.

133. Describe how to join a motorway (six points).

134. Studs on the motorway have various colours

depending on their purpose. What are the colours of the studs in the following locations:
a) The left-hand side of the carriageway.
b) The right-hand side of the carriageway.
c) The line separating the acceleration and deceleration lanes from the through carriageway.

135. At motorway road works you should leave a safe gap to the car in front. What two things may be different about the road?

136. Can you reverse your car on the motorway?

137. Except when overtaking, you must drive in the left-hand lane on motorways with ...
a) Three lanes.
b) Two lanes.
   TRUE or *FALSE*?

138. What five things must you do when you want to overtake on the motorway?

139. Where are you allowed to let your vehicle stand on the motorway if you break down?

140. On which side of the motorway will you find the exit slip road that takes you back to the 'ordinary' road system?

141. What lighted signal would you expect to find on an overhead panel on the motorway telling you to leave the motorway at the next exit?

MOTORWAYS AND PRIMARY ROADS

142. It is important that you regularly look at your speedometer when leaving the motorway or using link roads. Why?

143. You have broken down on the motorway and have managed to get your car onto the hard shoulder. How do you find the nearest telephone in order to inform the authorities?

144. The distances to exits from the motorway are indicated by panels showing three, then two, then one white bar in a rectangular light blue panel. How many yards to the exit does each white bar represent?

145. On a motorway, an overhead signal in your lane shows a lighted arrow pointing diagonally downwards to the left. What does this mean?

146. Traffic on motorways is fast, so what must you do before joining, and while on the motorway?

Primary Routes and Local Roads

147. Describe the road markings which indicate the edges of lanes on the road.

148. How do you move your arm when signalling that you want to move out or turn to the right?

149. What are you indicating when you extend your arm and move it rapidly up and down?

PASS YOUR HIGHWAY CODE TEST

150. A police officer is directing the traffic. You signal to the officer by showing him the palm of your upraised left hand. What are you saying about your driving intentions?

151. What does it signify if a police officer directing traffic faces the traffic with his arm straight up?

152. At a road junction, the traffic lights have turned green. What does this mean?

153. You want to make a right turn from a main road. However, another vehicle coming from the opposite direction, also wishes to do so. This means you will have to pass the other vehicle as you prepare to make your own right turn. When passing the other vehicle, should you keep it to your left or to your right?

154. Where should you wait when turning right from a dual carriageway?

155. In which of the following circumstances, if any, are you allowed to overtake on the *LEFT-HAND SIDE*?
    a) On dual carriageways at normal speeds.
    b) When someone ahead is signalling right.
    c) When a queue of traffic in a lane to your right is moving more slowly than you are.
    d) If you want to turn left.

MOTORWAYS AND PRIMARY ROADS

156. What can you deduce from the fact that red and amber traffic lights are showing together?

157. An eight-sided, red sign says STOP in white letters. A white, red-edged, inverted triangle says GIVE WAY in black letters. What do these two road signs have in common and what do they mean?

158. A roundabout has four exits. You wish to take the third. At what points should you indicate your intention?

159. Can you reverse from a side road into a main road?

160. What is the purpose of giving signals while driving? What three things should you remember to do?

161. You are driving slowly and carefully along a narrow, winding road. There is a great deal of oncoming traffic. A faster vehicle than yours comes up behind you and wants to overtake. What should you do?

162. When should you use your fog lamps?

163. When must a passenger in the rear wear a seat belt?

164. What is a crawler lane?

165. What does a single line of long markings with short gaps, along the middle of the road, mean?

PASS YOUR HIGHWAY CODE TEST

166. Out in the countryside, you are driving along a narrow single-track road when a vehicle comes towards you. There is a passing place at this point, but it is not on your side of the road. What should you do?

167. At a junction leading into a main road where there are broken white lines in front of your car, in which road do vehicles have the right of way?

168. On a three-lane dual carriageway, what is the purpose of the right-hand lane?

169. In what circumstances are you allowed to drive in the centre lane on a three-lane dual carriageway, and for how long?

170. You are driving along a one-way street and wish to turn off it at the next exit on the right. How do you prepare for this manoeuvre?

171. If you have to move from one lane to another on the road, which of the following must you normally do before starting this manoeuvre?
    a) First accelerate.
    b) First glance in your mirror.
    c) Sound your horn.
    d) Use your signal indicators.

172. On a single carriageway or undivided road, where there are three lanes, which lane is used ...
    a) For overtaking?
    b) For right turns?

MOTORWAYS AND PRIMARY ROADS

173. If you are driving a slow vehicle on a narrow road, and there is a queue of cars behind you, what should you do?

174. You must stop if the police tell you to. How will they tell you?

175. What should you not do in a traffic jam?

176. Unless signs or markings say otherwise, which lanes must you not use on a four-lane single carriageway?

177. What is the right hand lane of a two-lane dual carriageway for?

Section Five
You and Your Car

178. At what age is a young person legally responsible for wearing their seat belt?

179. You have a well-behaved and obedient dog in the car with you. Can you let it out on a road without a lead?

180. In an estate car or hatchback, where should children not be allowed to sit?

181. If your car is fitted with L-plates, perhaps while a friend or relative is occasionally using it to learn how to drive, what should you do when your car is *NOT* being used for learning or practising?

182. Who is required *by law* to wear a seat belt (or appropriate restraint if a child) when travelling by car?

183. What are the most important requirements in choosing an approved 'child-restraint' or seat belt?

184. A child-restraint or seat belt is one protection you can give a youngster travelling by car. Can you think of another?

YOU AND YOUR CAR

185. You wish to warn other road users of your presence. Which two methods are open to you for this purpose?

186. You should not drive a car while under the influence of alcohol or drugs. Name two other conditions of health or lack of well-being which make it inadvisable to drive.

187. The headlamps on your car should always be properly adjusted. Name the principal *SAFETY* reason for this.

188. A police officer is controlling the traffic and you wish to tell him that you want to drive straight on. How do you do this?

189. What should you do if you become tired on a long journey and your concentration begins to falter?

190. You are driving along the road and want to turn right. You glance into your rear-view mirror and see that it is safe to turn right, then, just as you are preparing to make the manoeuvre, you realise you have forgotten to do something. What is it?

191. You have parked by the side of the road, in the correct position. You have made sure the handbrake is on firmly and that the engine and headlamps are switched off. What else should you do to ensure the safety of your car?

192. There are nine items in your car to which you should give particular attention. According to the

Highway Code, they must be in first-class condition at all times. Six of these items are lights, brakes, steering, seat belts, de-misters and washers. What are the other three?

193. You have parked your car. What must you do before you open the door to get out?

194. Are you allowed to park for a few minutes where you normally shouldn't, if you switch on your hazard warning lights?

195. Your car has broken down, at night, on the motorway. You manage to get your car to the hard shoulder, then get out your reflecting red triangle warning sign and place it 50 metres away from your car. You telephone the police, but when they arrive, they look at the warning sign and frown. What have you done wrong?

196. Which of your car's facilities should you especially use when driving in fog?

197. Who do you ask about whether you can drive when taking a medicine that is ...
a) Prescribed?
b) Not prescribed?

198. You must be able to read (with glasses if needed) a number plate at what distance?

199. When should you NOT wear tinted glasses?

YOU AND YOUR CAR

200. What are the qualifications for supervising a learner driver?

201. You should not drink and drive, even if you are still below the legal limit. What four things does alcohol affect?

202. When can you use a telephone while driving?

Section Six
Markings on the Road

203. What road marking indicates a bus stop?

204. How are directions indicated by road markings?

205. You see KEEP CLEAR painted on the road in tall white letters. What is it that you must keep clear?

206. A road marking consists of zigzag yellow lines. Written between the lines are three words.
    .... KEEP CLEAR
    What is the first word and what does the road marking indicate?

PASS YOUR HIGHWAY CODE TEST

207. What type of roundabout has (at places where you must give way to traffic already on it) a line of small, box-shaped rectangles painted on the road?

208. There are two kinds of STOP lines painted across the carriageway. One is for stopping at a STOP sign. The other is for stopping at traffic signals or a police control. How do these two stop lines differ?

209. Yellow lines painted over the kerb are accompanied by an explanatory plate nearby. How many lines would you expect to see on the kerb if the plate forbad the following.
    a) Loading at any time.
    b) Loading Monday to Thursday, 9.30 a.m. - 4.30 p.m.
    c) Loading after 8.30 a.m. or before 6.30 p.m. on working days, including Saturdays.

210. Describe the road markings which indicate the edges of driving lanes.

211. You are in a side road, waiting to enter the main road and, of course, you are giving way to the traffic on the main road, though if it had been clear you would not have had to stop. There are markings on the road to tell you where to wait. Describe them.

212. Yellow lines indicate certain restrictions. What type of restrictions are indicated by yellow lines

MARKINGS ON THE ROAD

painted on the road and what type by yellow lines painted on the kerb?

213. Two types of yellow line marking are used to indicate No Waiting for at least eight hours between 7 a.m. and 7 p.m. on four or more days. One comprises a single yellow line, the other a double yellow line. Which of these two *ALSO* prohibits waiting during additional periods?

214. Describe the normal markings which indicate the centre of the road.

215. You see a white triangle with a thick base and the triangle point facing towards you, painted on the road. What lies ahead?

216. When white diagonal stripes or white chevrons are painted on the road, their purpose is . . .
a) To separate streams of traffic on the road.
b) To indicate overtaking areas.
c) To indicate where traffic may turn right.

217. Under what circumstances are you permitted to cross a double white line when the line nearer to you is a *solid* one?
a) When overtaking.
b) When moving out of premises or a side road.
c) To avoid a stationary obstruction in the road.
d) None.

218. Of the two lines in the centre of the road, the broken white line is nearer to you. Can you overtake here and so cross the white lines?

35

PASS YOUR HIGHWAY CODE TEST

219. What road markings indicate the approach to a Zebra crossing?

220. Roads may have coloured reflective studs embedded in them. What is indicated by studs in the following colours?
    a) Amber.
    b) Red.
    c) White.
    d) Green.

221. You are in the zigzag area of a Zebra crossing and you want to overtake. Are you allowed to?

222. You would obviously not drive across a Zebra crossing while pedestrians are actually on it, but can you drive over it when pedestrians are at the kerb by the crossing?

223. On the motorway, what is indicated by green studs embedded in the road surface?

224. On the motorway, what is indicated by red studs embedded in the road surface?

225. Chevrons painted in the road have a solid white-edged line. Are you allowed to drive over them at any time?

226. What do yellow criss-cross lines in the road mean?

Section Seven
Signs on the Road

227. Describe the shape of the majority of warning signs you may see on the road.

228. A round, white, red-edged sign shows the figure of a man walking. What does this sign denote?

229. There are two arrows in a triangular sign which indicate that there is two-way traffic going across a one-way road. Describe the two arrows.

230. When a sign shows red, amber and green traffic lights in a vertical rectangle, with a red bar diagonally across them, what does this mean?

231. A white, red-edged sign shows two cars, a black one on the left, a red one on the right. What does this mean?

232. What sign, in the form of a diamond-shaped panel, must be carried by vehicles loaded with spontaneously combustible materials?

233. Vehicles with loads that overhang the front or rear by more than 1.83 metres must carry projection markers with red- and white-slanted stripes. They come in two shapes . . .

PASS YOUR HIGHWAY CODE TEST

    a) A long, right-angled triangle.
    b) An isosceles triangle (i.e. with sides of equal length) pointing downwards.
Which of them is carried on the *SIDE* of the vehicle and which at the *REAR*?

234. Where are you likely to see a panel showing alternating flashing red light signals, indicating that you must stop?

235. What is the nature of the majority of circular signs with red edges?

236. When a circular blue sign shows a bicycle on the left and an adult and child pedestrians on the right, what does this mean?

237. A stretch of road has, firstly, a blue sign showing '30' written in white. Further on, there is another sign — the same one, in fact, but with a red diagonal bar across the '30'. What do the two signs mean?

238. Which circular blue road sign contains the following?
    a) Two arrows.
    b) Three arrows.

239. Two triangular, red-edged signs indicate a level crossing ahead. One of them contains the silhouette of a gate. The other contains the

SIGNS ON THE ROAD

silhouette of a steam engine. What is the chief difference between level crossings displaying one or other of these signs?

240. What does the silhouette of an aircraft mean on a road sign, and what *shape* is the sign?

241. Describe the colours in which you may expect to find direction signs on non-primary routes, such as B roads?

242. How does a road sign tell you that it indicates a 'Ring Road'?

243. What is the significance of a yellow panel printed with a black motif — an arrowhead pointing left or right?

244. What is indicated by white arrows on a blue background when they are displayed on a long black panel over a motorway?

245. A white, red-edged, round sign shows the outline of a car front. Does this mean that no vehicles are allowed on the road?

246. How does a road sign indicate an unspecified danger lying ahead?

247. What can you infer from a triangular, red-edged road sign showing a deer in silhouette?

PASS YOUR HIGHWAY CODE TEST

248. Describe the information sign indicating a parking meter zone.

249. What is the import of a flashing amber signal, placed below the sign which indicates children going to and from school?

250. A road has four lanes. There are four, small, box panels placed over the road which indicate that two of the lanes are open and the other two closed. What would you expect to find displayed in the box panels?

251. Describe the sign which indicates a parking place for caravans.

252. What does a large white 'H' on a light blue background denote when displayed on a road sign?

253. A sign on a motorway shows two white bars in a rectangular light blue panel. How far is the sign from the next motorway exit?

254. A rectangular road sign with a pale blue background shows a 'T' shape motif. The vertical shaft of the 'T' is painted in white, the cross-bar of the 'T' in red. What does this mean?

SIGNS ON THE ROAD

255. Describe the roadside sign on a three-lane motorway which means RIGHT-HAND LANE CLOSED.

256. Describe the overhead motorway sign which means END OF RESTRICTION.

257. The overhead signal above your lane on the motorway is flashing a set of red lights. What should you do?

258. What is signified by flashing red lights showing on a level crossing?

259. A large, white, square road sign has a white 'P' on the left-hand side, enclosed in a light blue square. What does the rest of the sign say? (Three words.)

260. What can you expect to see in a long, horizontal black road sign which indicates a sharp bend in the road to the left?

261. How is a level crossing that does not have a barrier indicated?

262. What sign indicates a roundabout ahead?

263. Name five triangular, red-edged signs which show silhouettes of people.

264. A triangular, red-edged sign on a road shows two parallel lines which kink inwards, towards each other. What does this mean?

PASS YOUR HIGHWAY CODE TEST

265. Two blue signs on the road feature arrows pointing straight up. One blue sign is round, the other is rectangular. What does each signify?

Section Eight
Roundabouts and Level Crossings

266. What may cyclists, motorcyclists and horse riders do on a roundabout?

267. What should you watch out for at mini roundabouts?

268. Some junctions have more than one roundabout. How should you act at these junctions?

269. Who has the right of way on a roundabout?

270. What is the first thing you must do as you approach a roundabout?

271. How do you turn left at a roundabout?

272. What should you remember about long vehicles at a roundabout?

273. How do you turn right or go full circle at a roundabout?

274. If there are two lanes at the entrance to a roundabout, for *what purpose* do you approach in . . .
a) The left-hand lane?
b) The right-hand lane?

PASS YOUR HIGHWAY CODE TEST

275. At a level crossing without signals, the barrier starts to close as you approach. What should you do?

276. At an automatic level crossing, you find amber lights followed by flashing red STOP lights. You of course halt and let the train that is on the line pass over the crossing. Once it has gone, however, the lights continue to flash. Should you drive over the crossing at this juncture?

277. You must approach and cross a level crossing with care. What three things should you remember while crossing?

278. A level crossing has an automatic barrier across the left-hand side of the road only. What must you never do?

279. Certain level crossings have no gates or barriers, no attendants or red lights, but they *do* have a sign. What does the sign say?

280. Half-barrier level crossings have three signals, apart from the barriers lowering, indicating that vehicles must stop at the crossing. Amber lights and flashing red STOP lights are two of these signals. What is the third?

281. What should you do if you break down or have an accident on a level crossing?

282. On which type of level crossing would you expect to find a barrier with red and white vertical stripes?

ROUNDABOUTS AND LEVEL CROSSINGS

283. You see, from a sign on the road, that there is a level crossing ahead. The sign shows a steam engine in silhouette. What type of level crossing is ahead?

284. What type of sign is for train drivers only?

285. At level crossings which have gates, but no signals or attendant, what do you do?

286. What sign on the road indicates that there is a roundabout ahead?

287. A triangular, red-edged sign at a level crossing shows the silhouette of a gate. What type of crossing is this?

288. What sign would you expect to see at a level crossing without a barrier?

289. Describe the sign for Trams Crossing Ahead.

290. May you enter a lane reserved for trams?

291. You are in the course of going over a level crossing when the amber warning lights on the crossing start to show, or you hear the alarm. What should you do?
    a) Reverse your car off the crossing.
    b) Stay where you are.
    c) Drive forwards off the crossing.

292. When there are more than three lanes at the entrance to a roundabout, which one do you approach in?

PASS YOUR HIGHWAY CODE TEST

293. Once on the roundabout, which lane should you use to drive on and round it?

294. How do you go straight ahead at a roundabout?

295. You enter a roundabout and want to take the first exit from it. What signal do you give and when do you give it?

296. Assuming that it is clear for you to do so, in what lane on the road should you approach a roundabout?

297. In what circumstances will you signal, firstly, *RIGHT* and then *LEFT*, on a roundabout?

298. What warning signal at a level crossing tells you that a train is approaching?

299. At an 'open' level crossing, that is, one without gates or barriers, you should make sure that no trains are approaching by listening for the sound of a train and *two* other actions. What are these?

300. What MUST you remember about parking and trams?

301. If you are driving a large and/or slow-moving vehicle and wish to traverse a level crossing, how do you ensure that it is safe to do so?

ROUNDABOUTS AND LEVEL CROSSINGS

302. You should look out for pedestrians at tram stops. What else MUST you do at tram stops ...
    a) With platforms?
    b) Without platforms?

303. Where should you be especially careful of trams?

304. How do you cross a level crossing, where there are gates and small red-green traffic lights?

305. When on a roundabout, other vehicles will cross in front of you when taking exits before your own. What should you do when this occurs?

Section Nine
Parking and Waiting

306. There is a parked vehicle in your lane a short way ahead of you. Another vehicle is coming towards you from the opposite direction. Should you move out and drive past the parked vehicle or not?

307. Disabled persons are entitled to certain parking concessions such as specially designated bays in multi-storey car parks which serve a supermarket. Disabled drivers must display a badge in their car so that other drivers will recognise them. What colour is the badge and can anyone else park in the space?

PASS YOUR HIGHWAY CODE TEST

308. A mobile shop or ice-cream van is parked at the roadside and is serving customers. What or who must you watch out for in these circumstances when driving along this road?

309. Where can you park your car on a motorway?

310. May you park at night in a 30 mph road, pointing against the direction of the traffic flow?

311. You may not park within 10 metres (32 feet) of a junction unless in . . . ?

312. Should you park near a school entrance or on the approach to a level crossing?

313. Apart from not parking in one, what must you remember about tram lanes?

314. Where should vehicles not wait or park because it is difficult for other road users to see the road clearly?

315. Goods vehicles with a maximum laden weight over 7.5 tonnes can only be parked on a verge or footway when loading, and then there is another rule to be obeyed. What is it?

316. It is not permitted to park opposite a traffic island in the middle of a road. Why?

317. You should avoid parking on the road in fog, but if you can't you should . . . ?

PARKING AND WAITING

318. You have parked your car by the side of the road. Before you or your passengers open the door to get out, what must you check on the road itself?

319. You must not park your vehicle opposite or nearly opposite a stationary vehicle on the other side of the road if . . . ?

320. Before leaving your vehicle parked by the road, you should switch off the engine and headlamps and lock the car. What else needs to be done?

321. Under certain conditions when motorbikes, cars, goods vehicles up to 1,525 kg unladen and invalid carriages can be parked at night without lights on roads, what must be the speed limit: 50 mph or less, or 20 mph or less, or 30 mph or less?

322. When parking near a road junction, at what minimum distance should you do so: 5 metres (16 feet), or 15 metres (48 feet), or 10 metres (32 feet)?

323. When may you stop on an urban clearway during its period of operation?

324. May you park in the following places?
    a) In the area of zigzag lines on either side of a pedestrian crossing.
    b) On a clearway at the weekend.
    c) In a bus, tram or cycle lane outside its period of operation.
    d) Where the centre of the road has double white lines.

PASS YOUR HIGHWAY CODE TEST

325. *TRUE* or *FALSE*? You may park your vehicle:
   a) In front of an entrance.
   b) On the left-hand side of the road at night.
   c) On a footpath or pavement.

326. You have parked your car and your dog is anxious to get out. So you open the door and let him leap onto the pavement. What have you done wrong?

327. The plate which indicates that one may *NEVER* wait at a certain spot consists of a light blue, red-edged circle with a red, diagonal bar on a yellow background. Below the circle is some lettering. What does it say?

328. Where there are waiting restrictions, the plates displayed to indicate this state of affairs may have yellow or light blue backgrounds. Which one of these backgrounds tells you when limited waiting is permitted?

329. In certain places you will see yellow lines painted over the edge of the kerb. What type of restriction does this indicate?

330. Where are yellow lines painted in order to denote that there are waiting restrictions?

331. If you see three yellow lines painted over a kerb, what restriction does this indicate?

332. One yellow line painted over the kerb indicates loading restrictions when?

PARKING AND WAITING

333. Apart from yellow lines, what may be marked along the edge of the road to indicate parking restrictions?

334. You may park on the slip road leading to a motorway. *TRUE* or *FALSE*?

335. You may park on the central reservation of a motorway. *TRUE* or *FALSE*?

336. Where can you find out when parking restrictions apply?

337. What MUST a vehicle with a projecting load have when parked at night?

338. When should you use a parking space off the road, rather than a space by the kerb?

339. You can't park on a level crossing, but may you park near it?

340. If the pavement alongside a road is very wide — say four or five times wider than the normal pavement — are you allowed to park on it or let your vehicle wait there?

341. At which of the following places can you park?
 a) At bus stops.
 b) In a taxi rank.
 c) In a layby.
 d) Where the kerb has been lowered for wheelchair users.

PASS YOUR HIGHWAY CODE TEST

342. Where is it safest to get out of a parked car?

343. What should you do if you park next to a vehicle which has a disabled person's badge?

344. When parking by the roadside, where should you position your car?

345. May you park in a passing place on a single track road?

Section Ten
Breakdowns, Accidents and Mishaps

346. If your vehicle breaks down and refuses to move while you are on the road, what is your first priority?

347. At the scene of an accident, what eight things should you do?

BREAKDOWNS

348. In the event of a breakdown, how far away from your vehicle should you place your reflecting, red triangle warning sign?
a) On a motorway.
b) On an ordinary road.

349. What three things may warn you of an accident ahead?

350. Your car has broken down at night. As you stand around waiting for the emergency service van to arrive, where should you *NOT* place yourself?

351. What two pieces of vital information must the police have when being told of an accident?

352. You find a motorcyclist lying in the road after an accident. Should you remove his helmet to get a look at his injuries?

353. How is a vehicle carrying dangerous goods marked when it has them in ...
a) Packages?
b) Tanks?

354. As well as the normal actions at the scene of an accident, what extra things must you do when there are vehicles carrying dangerous goods?

355. In accidents involving vehicles carrying dangerous goods, why do drivers and others at the scene need to test the direction of the wind when the dangerous goods are liquids and have spilled onto the carriageway?

PASS YOUR HIGHWAY CODE TEST

356. If your car breaks down on a motorway, where should you place it, if it is possible to move it?

357. The car in front of you has its roof rack loaded with a small boat. Suddenly, a gust of wind rocks the boat and a paddle falls out of it onto the motorway. The driver of the car brakes briefly, as if to stop, then changes his mind and indicates that he is moving left into the next, inner, lane. He parks his car on the hard shoulder and goes to the nearest telephone. The paddle, of course, is still lying on the motorway, a hazard to all traffic that passes by. Has the driver of the car in front done the right thing in leaving it there?

358. What should you do if something falls from your vehicle on an ordinary road?

359. An accident has happened on the other carriageway. Is it ok for you to slow down and have a look as you pass?

360. If you break down on a motorway, where should you and your passengers . . .
    a) Enter and leave the vehicle?
    b) Wait?

361. On the motorway, there are telephones to call emergency services from, every mile along the hard shoulder. What two things should you remember about finding one of these phones?

362. What four things should you do if you break down on a motorway and can't get to the hard shoulder?

BREAKDOWNS

363. If you break down on a motorway, and a disability stops you carrying out the normal procedures, what should you do?

364. How should you rejoin the carriageway after a breakdown on the motorway?

Section Eleven
First Aid on the Road

First Aid in road accidents (pages 75 and 76 of the Highway Code) is something to be undertaken with caution. Unless you are a trained First Aider, you must take exceptional care in situations which can be as distressing as they are unfamiliar to you. Someone else's life can literally be in your hands and if you genuinely feel unable to cope with the situation it is best to confine yourself to comforting and reassuring accident victims. You can also apply yourself to other non-medical aid. The answers to Questions 366 to 369 and 372 will tell you what constitutes this type of aid.

If you shrink from giving First Aid as specified in the Highway Code, please do not consider yourself inadequate. You are not only dealing with an unfamiliar situation, but may yourself be a victim of shock which can impair your ability to take the correct action.

PASS YOUR HIGHWAY CODE TEST

Your best procedure is to prepare yourself for the eventuality which, as stated in the Highway Code, comprises carrying a First Aid Kit (and knowing how to use it) and learning First Aid. Instruction in First Aid is given by the St. John Ambulance Association and Brigade, St. Andrew's Ambulance Association and the British Red Cross Society.

365. After an accident, the possibility of further collisions from oncoming traffic is mentioned in the Highway Code as one of two threatened dangers. What is the other?

366. After an accident, an ambulance should be called as soon as possible and the ambulance services given information as to the number of vehicles and casualties involved. What else is vital for the ambulance services to know?

367. Why is a ban on smoking in the area of a road accident an important one?

368. Someone at the scene of an accident has a thermos flask of tea and wants to give one of the casualties a drink from it. Is this wise?

369. A casualty in the passenger seat of a car that has been in an accident asks for help in getting out. Should you or should you not agree?

370. What is the first thing you should do for an accident victim whose breathing has stopped?

FIRST AID ON THE ROAD

371. After taking the action detailed in the answer to Question 370 above, in which direction should you keep the victim's head tilted as a preliminary to giving mouth-to-mouth resuscitation: backwards, to one side, or forwards?

372. Why should you make sure that an accident victim is not left alone or allowed to become cold?

373. You have decided to give mouth-to-mouth resuscitation. What is your first action?

374. In mouth-to-mouth resuscitation, how do you know that your efforts are having effect?

375. An accident victim has suffered a wound and is bleeding. What should you use to help control the bleeding?

376. Through mouth-to-mouth resuscitation, you have managed to get an accident victim breathing. At what intervals should you again apply this method until the casualty can breathe unaided?

Section Twelve
Road Junctions and Traffic Lights

377. If you are about to turn into a road at a junction but you see some pedestrians crossing it, what should you do?

378. The light signals at a pedestrian crossing show green, indicating that you may drive on. When should you *NOT* do so, despite what the light signals say?

379. You are on the motorway and you see direction signs over the road. What should you do, and what should you be careful of?

380. Can you overtake at a road junction?

381. The road on which you are travelling is a local road and you are approaching a main road at the junction ahead. What can you expect to find at the point where your road meets the main road, and what should you do?

382. What may different lanes at junctions do?

383. What is a box junction?

ROAD JUNCTIONS

384. At a box junction, you want to turn right. The exit is clear but the oncoming traffic is too heavy and there are other vehicles waiting to do the same as you. In these circumstances, you may not enter the box. *TRUE* or *FALSE*?

385. What is the procedure for turning right? There are seven points.

386. When an amber light shows at the traffic lights, what is it 'telling' you?

387. What is the purpose of the green filter arrow which often accompanies sets of traffic lights, and what must you NOT do?

388. If you come to a set of traffic lights just as the red and amber lights show together, should you stop or drive on?

389. Why must you be extra careful when turning right into a main road?

390. What is the procedure for turning left? There are five points.

391. A road sign tells you that the traffic lights ahead are not operating. What is on this sign, and what should you do?

392. You are waiting to go straight ahead at traffic lights at a road junction. The green GO light shows, but vehicles in front of you are at the centre of the junction, queuing up to turn right. Should you move off from the traffic lights?

PASS YOUR HIGHWAY CODE TEST

393. You should take extra care at junctions. Which two sets of road users should you particularly look out for, and what are the reasons?

394. If you see a road sign which shows a road as a straight, upright, black line with a short, red bar across the top, does this mean that there is a 'T' junction ahead?

395. A car pulls into the central reservation of a dual carriageway. What is the driver's intention?

396. At a set of traffic lights, the main signals show Red and Amber, with a green arrow filter sign also showing to the left. Are you permitted to drive straight on?

397. What must you do if you want to turn left over a bus, cycle, or tram lane?

398. Traffic lights on ordinary roads which show the amber light only mean STOP at the stop line, but there are two circumstances in which you may drive on. What are they?

399. Name three forms of traffic light signals — single lights or two lights showing together — which mean STOP.

400. What is the difference between a double, broken white line painted on a road where it meets another at a junction, and a solid white line painted at the same place?

Section Thirteen
Three Driver's Tales

The Road

One moment the sky overhead seemed clear with little more than a light overcast, the next, David found to his fury that he had driven into a patch of heavy rain. He cursed quietly to himself as he glanced at the sky ahead and saw the grey-black clouds which denoted yet more rain further along the road.

'Just my rotten luck', David grimaced. 'An important appointment and I'm running late already.' He glanced at his speedometer. It showed forty miles an hour.

David reckoned the grip of his wheels on the road through the feel of his steering wheel.

'Seems okay,' he thought. 'Forty is all right.' Maybe he would be on time after all, or not too late at any rate.

Just then, out of the corner of his left eye, David noticed a car overtaking him. It speeded past, cut smartly in front of David, accelerated a bit and presented him with an infuriating view of its boot and rear window barely thirty metres in front of him.

David cursed again, this time aloud. He felt a tremendous urge to swerve to the right, overtake this fellow and teach him a lesson!

PASS YOUR HIGHWAY CODE TEST

Questions

A. What cardinal error — both very dangerous and illegal — was made by the driver of the overtaking car?

B. What further error did this driver make when moving into the space in front of David's car?

C. Was the distance between David's car and the overtaking car a safe one in the road conditions then prevailing?

D. Having been so abruptly overtaken, should David overtake in his turn? If not, what should he do?

Other Road Users

'Cheerio, love!' David gave his wife Anne a parting kiss and hugged their three children before getting into his car. He fastened his seat belt, gave a smile and a wave and drove off.

'Lucky old David,' Anne thought, as she watched him go. 'He doesn't have to take the kids to school before going to work, like I do.'

The three children piled into the back of their mother's car. 'Okay, kids,' Anne told them, 'here we go again.'

Anne started up and headed for the familiar route that led towards the school. She was nearing the junction where, normally, she drove straight on, when ten-year-old Elizabeth piped up: 'Mummy, look! There's a hole in the road and some men working there! Drive past it so we can have a look, please do!'

THREE DRIVER'S TALES

'Don't be silly, Elizabeth,' Anne told her. 'The road's closed — can't you see the sign? We'll have to make a diversion.'

The diversion made, Anne found herself driving along an unfamiliar road. There seemed to be a lot of pedestrians about. They were going to delay her, Anne thought, feeling flustered and impatient.

Zigzag lines on the road showed her that a Zebra crossing was ahead. She prepared to slow down and, opening her window, made a hand signal to the three pedestrians waiting by the kerb, extending her arm and making a circular movement with it.

The pedestrians just stared at her, looking confused. They hovered on the pavement, as if unsure of what to do.

'What's the matter with them?' Anne was becoming annoyed. 'Why won't they cross the road?'

Questions

E. Anne and her children omitted something important after getting in their car. What was it?

F. Apart from signs telling Anne that the road ahead was closed, and the diversion signs, what other warning sign might she have seen?

G. Where were the zigzag lines indicating a Zebra crossing painted on the road surface?

H. Why were the pedestrians reluctant to cross at the Zebra crossing after seeing Anne's signal?

PASS YOUR HIGHWAY CODE TEST

Driving Conditions and Night Driving

The evening at the theatre had been fun. Now David, with Anne beside him, was enjoying the drive home through almost empty night-time streets.

A cat darted across the road in front of the car, and instinctively David sounded the horn.

'You could get had up for that,' Anne teased him.
'No I can't,' said David. 'Look at your watch!'
Anne did so. 'You sounded that horn with only three minutes to spare, you know. Hey! I just saw three of those street lamps go out. It's pretty murky now.'

She was right. Visibility wasn't good now, so David switched from side lights to dipped headlights.

At the junction David prepared to turn into the side road that led home. Before turning, he slowed and glanced at the entrance to the side road.

'You know that road where we saw the cat,' said Anne, 'I counted ten cars parked at my side of the road, and six of them weren't parked properly.'

Questions

I. At what time did David sound his car horn?

J. Was David correct to alter his lights from side lights to dipped headlights?

K. Why did David scrutinise the entrance to the side road before driving down it?

L. What told Anne that six out of the ten parked cars were not parked correctly?

Section Fourteen
Traffic Signs

Colour is represented by the shading in the boxes opposite.

Red

Blue

SIGNS GIVING ORDERS

Maximum speed

National speed limit applies

Stop and Give Way

Give way to traffic on major road

No entry for vehicular traffic

No right turn

No left turn

No U turns

No motor vehicles

No motor vehicles except solo motorcyles, scooters or mopeds

Manually operated temporary 'STOP' sign

No vehicles with over 12 seats except regular scheduled school and works buses

No goods vehicles over maximum gross weight shown (in tonnes)

No stopping (Clearway)

Axle weight limit in tonnes

No vehicles over height shown

School crossing patrol

No vehicles

No overtaking

Give priority to vehicles from opposite direction

PASS YOUR HIGHWAY CODE TEST

No cycling

No pedestrians

No vehicle or combination of vehicles over length shown

No vehicles over width shown

Parking restricted to use by people named on sign

No stopping during times shown except for as long as necessary to set down or pick up passengers

Entry to a 20 mph zone

Plates below some signs qualify their message

Exception for regular scheduled, school and work buses

End of restriction

Exception for access to premises and land adjacent to the road where there is no alternative route

Exception for loading/unloading goods

Blue backgrounds

Turn left ahead (right if symbol reversed)

End of minimum speed

Turn left (right if symbol reversed)

Keep left (right if symbol reversed)

Segregated pedal cycle and pedestrian zone

Ahead only

Minimum speed

Vehicles may pass either side to reach same destination

One-way traffic (Note: compare circular 'Ahead only' sign)

Route to be used by pedal cycles only

With-flow pedal cycle lane

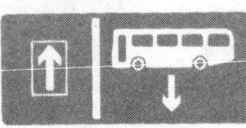

Contra-flow bus lane

With-flow bus and cycle lane

Mini-roundabout (roundabout circulation - give way to vehicles from the immediate right)

TRAFFIC SIGNS

WARNING SIGNS

Dual carriageway ends

Slippery road

Two-way traffic straight ahead

Two-way traffic crosses one-way road

Road narrows on right (left if symbol reversed)

Road narrows on both sides

Traffic merges from left

Traffic merges from right

Road works

Hump bridge

Junction on bend ahead

Loose chippings

Steep hill downwards

Steep hill upwards

Gradients may be shown as a ratio i.e. 20% = 1:5

Level crossing with barrier or gate ahead

Level crossing without barrier or gate ahead

Double bend first to left (symbol may be reversed)

Plate below some signs

Sharp deviation of route to left (or right if chevrons reversed)

Bend to right (or left if symbol reversed)

Low-flying aircraft or sudden aircraft noise

Uneven road

Traffic signals

Failure of traffic light signals

PASS YOUR HIGHWAY CODE TEST

Available width of headroom indicated

Trams crossing ahead

Falling or fallen rocks

Distance to 'STOP' line ahead

Distance to 'Give Way' line ahead

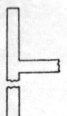

Light signals ahead at level crossing, airfield or bridge

Distance to tunnel

Pedestrians in road ahead

Distance over which road humps extend

Elderly people (or blind or disabled as shown) crossing road

Level crossing without barrier

Children going to or from school

School crossing patrol ahead (Some signs have amber lights which flash when children are crossing

Overhead electric cable; plate indicates maximum height of vehicles which can pass safely

Other danger plate indicates nature of danger

Risk of grounding of long low vehicles at level crossing

Accompanied horses or ponies crossing the road ahead

68

TRAFFIC SIGNS

- Crossroads
- Roundabout 
- T-junction 
- Staggered junction 
- Cycle route ahead 
- Worded warning sign 
- Opening or swing bridge ahead 
- Quayside or river bank 
- Pedestrian crossing 
- Cattle 
- Wild animals 
- Wild horses or ponies 

DIRECTION SIGNS
Primary Routes — Green backgrounds

Scarborough A64
Pickering A169
York A64

On approaches to junctions

A46
Lincoln 12
Newark 28
(Nottingham 48)
Leicester 63

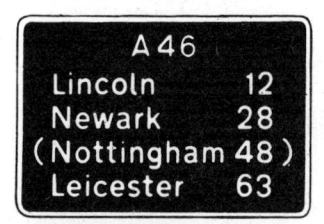

Route confirmatory sign after junction

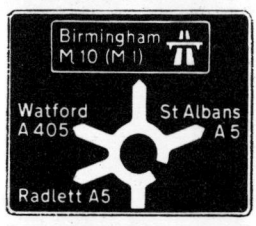

Birmingham M10 (M1)
Watford A405
St Albans A5
Radlett A5

On approaches to junctions (The blue panel indicates that the motorway commences from the junction ahead. The motorway shown in brackets can also be reached by proceeding in that direction)

Sutton C'field A38
Tamworth (A4091)

At the junction

R

Ring road

PASS YOUR HIGHWAY CODE TEST

DIRECTION SIGNS
Motorways — Blue backgrounds

Start of motorway and point from which motorway regulations apply

End of motorway

On approaches to junctions (junction number on black background)

At a junction leading directly into a motorway

Route confirmatory sign after junction

The panel with the sloping arrow indicates the destinations which can be reached by leaving the motorway at the next junction

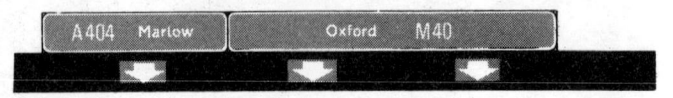

Downward pointing arrows mean 'Get in Lane'

TRAFFIC SIGNS

INFORMATION SIGNS

One-way street

Recommended route for pedal cycles

Tourist information point

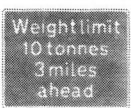

Advance warning of restriction or prohibition ahead

Parking place for towed caravans

Hospital ahead

No through road

Bus lane on road at junction ahead

End of controlled parking zone

Entrance to controlled parking zone

'Count-down' markers at exit from motorway (each bar represents 100 yards to the exit) Green-backed markers may be used on primary routes and white-backed markers with red bars on the approaches to concealed level crossings

Priority over vehicles from opposite direction

Temporary lane closure (the number and position of arrows and red bars may be varied according to the lanes open and closed)

Appropriate traffic lanes at junction ahead

71

Section Fifteen
The Theory Test

From mid 1996, the driving test will include a 40-minute theory test based on 35 multiple-choice questions. Complete these questions to give you an idea of whether you are ready for your theory test.

1. When being overtaken by another vehicle, you must:
   a) drive as close to the left as possible;
   b) always reduce speed;
   c) not accelerate;
   d) look in the mirror.

2. The main controls of a car are conveniently grouped together as:
   a) hand and foot;
   b) left to right;
   c) mechanical and visual;
   d) hand and visual.

3. The national speed limit on a dual carriageway is:
   a) 70 mph;
   b) 60 mph;
   c) 50 mph;
   d) 80 mph.

THE THEORY TEST

4. Setting down or picking up passengers on a motorway is:
   a) only permissible on slips roads;
   b) only permissible at weekends;
   c) only permissible on the hard shoulder;
   d) not permissible.

5. If another driver's bad manners or incompetence annoys, you should:
   a) teach him a lesson;
   b) flash your lights or sound your horn;
   c) do nothing other than set a good example;
   d) proceed with caution.

6. Route signs with green backgrounds are found:
   a) on motorways;
   b) on primary routes;
   c) on local routes;
   d) on single track lanes.

7. Driving in fog, you are advised to maintain a separation distance from the vehicle ahead:
   a) such that you can keep the car ahead in sight;
   b) which is equal to your overall stopping distance for your road speed;
   c) which is equal to your thinking distance for your road speed;
   d) to be able to stop within the distance you can see to be clear.

8. Is it safe to allow children to lie or sit in the rear of an estate or hatchback?
   a) yes, if they sit on a cushion;

PASS YOUR HIGHWAY CODE TEST

    b) no, except in special circumstances;
    c) yes, if your view to the rear is clear;
    d) no, not in any circumstances.

9. Having driven through a flooded road what should you check first?
    a) the ignition system is dry;
    b) no water has entered the exhaust pipe;
    c) your brakes;
    d) your lights and horn.

10. Car telephones may only be used:
    a) when on the move in an emergency;
    b) when you have found a safe place to stop;
    c) on the hard shoulder of a motorway;
    d) during breakdowns or accidents.

11. To supervise a learner driver you must: (Mark 2 answers)
    a) have held a full licence for at least 3 years;
    b) be at least 21;
    c) be an approved driving instructor;
    d) hold an advanced driving certificate.

12. When turning right into a narrow side road you should position your car before turning:
    a) well to the left;
    b) as close to the middle of the road as is safe;
    c) just right of the centre;
    d) well to the right.

13. A circular blue sign with the number '30' and a red diagonal bar indicates:

THE THEORY TEST

   a) end of restriction;
   b) end of minimum 30 mph speed limit;
   c) maximum speed 30 mph;
   d) the driver can only travel at 30 mph.

14. What driver actions are likely to increase fuel consumption? (Mark 2 answers)
    a) harsh or rapid acceleration;
    b) driving at a constant speed;
    c) carrying heavy loads or roof racks;
    d) not cleaning the windscreen and other windows.

15. The extreme right-hand lane of a four-lane motorway should only be used:
    a) for overtaking;
    b) by emergency vehicles;
    c) by car drivers;
    d) if your speed exceeds 60 mph.

16. At a school crossing point, the person controlling the crossing has stepped back onto the footpath and you notice a child about to cross the road. You should:
    a) drive on;
    b) give way to the child, if the controller has noticed;
    c) give way to the child;
    d) sound your horn and drive on.

17. You may normally overtake another vehicle on the left if:
    a) you can do so safely;
    b) you intend to stop on the left;

c) you intend to continue straight ahead and a driver to the right of you is positioned to turn right and is signalling right;
d) you change down through the gears first.

18. Red bordered white circular signs with a red diagonal bar usually indicate:
   a) end of traffic movement restrictions;
   b) traffic movement restrictions;
   c) no entry;
   d) no vehicles.

19. What are the requirements for carried or towed loads? (Mark 2 answers)
   a) loads must be secure and evenly spread;
   b) loads must not stick out dangerously;
   c) there are no load restrictions except for the gross carrying capacity of your vehicle;
   d) passengers don't count as loads.

20. Pulling into a garage you have to drive over a pavement. Who has priority?
   a) you have priority having given a signal;
   b) pedestrians have priority;
   c) you both have equal priority;
   d) neither of you have priority and must give way.

21. When may you use high intensity rear fog lights?
   a) at night;
   b) when visibility is reduced to less than 100 m;
   c) when raining during the daytime;
   d) when visibility is reduced to less than 400 m.

Answers

Section One: The Road

1. *No closer than the overall shortest stopping distance (i.e. thinking AND braking distance added together) relative to your car's speed — and then only in good road conditions.* (Rule 57)

2. *You must now reckon the safe gap between yourself and the vehicle in front as being between YOU and the car which has just overtaken you. You should therefore drop back so that the gap is the proper, safe one.* (Rule 57)

3. *No more than the distance which is within the range of your vision. At that distance, other cars, pedestrians and other features should be at least identifiable.* (Rules 57 & 58)

4. *a) 240 feet or 73 metres.*
   b) 120 feet or 36 metres.
   c) 75 feet or 23 metres. (Rule 57)

5. *a) 70 feet or 21 metres.*
   b) 50 feet or 15 metres.
   c) 30 feet or 9 metres. (Rule 57)

6. *80 feet or 24 metres.* (Rule 57)

7. *20 feet (6 metres) for THINKING, 20 feet (6 metres) for BRAKING.* (Rule 57)

PASS YOUR HIGHWAY CODE TEST

8. Give way to the bus if safe to do so. (Rule 79)

9. When driving in fog, it is vital to slow down to a safe speed. In addition, you should watch your speed indicator in order to check that you are not accelerating without being aware of it. It is, in any case, wise to check your speedometer occasionally even when driving in normal conditions. This habit, once established, makes it easier to make the checks when it is particularly important to do so. (Rule 58)

10. Cyclists on the road have a 'narrow' profile. They are therefore less easy for motorists and other road users to see. In the case of pedal cyclists, they are also slower than other road users. (Rule 52)

11. Sleepiness can be kept at bay by ensuring there is a good supply of fresh air in the car. (Rule 162)

12. At 40 mph. (Rule 57)

13. Do not speed up, since this will shorten the safe distance between yourself and the car in front of you. (Rule 58)

14. Leave a 4 second gap. (Rule 57)

15. When road signs or markings indicate that right-hand driving is allowed. You may also move to the right-hand side of the road when you intend to overtake or to turn right, and in addition, when you pass stationary vehicles or pedestrians on the road, as long as it is safe for you to do so. (Rule 49)

ANSWERS: THE ROAD

16. *Move out a sufficient distance to the right to keep your car well clear of vehicles and pedestrians.*
(Rule 70)

17. *Policemen, traffic wardens and officials in charge of school road-crossing patrols.* (Rule 47)

18. *Loads carried on or towed by vehicles must be secure, must not stick out, and must not overload the vehicle.* (Rule 29)

19. *Two lanes are open, i.e. those lanes running beneath the arrows.* (Page 54)

20. *There are five exits/entrances on this roundabout — the four indicated by the green direction sign and the road on which you are travelling.* (Page 61)

21. *'Ring Road.'* (Page 61)

22. *By white arrows painted on the road.* (Page 65)

23. *That there is a sharp bend to the right in the road just ahead. If the road is about to bend sharply to the left, the white chevrons will point to the left. It is advisable, if safe, to slow down on seeing the 'sharp bend' sign, since too much speed may pull your car into the opposite lane as you round the corner.* (Page 59)

24. a) *Stop at the stop line, but only if you are NOT already across the line, or if, by pulling up, you could cause an accident.* (Rule 114)
    b) *Stop. However, be aware that the green GO signal will follow quite soon.* (Rule 114)

PASS YOUR HIGHWAY CODE TEST

    c) *Stop if you are going to drive straight on, but GO if you are following the filter signal and turning left.* (Rule 115)

25. *When signalled to stop by a police officer or an emergency traffic sign, or by a flashing red light signal.* (Rule 179)

26. *The deceleration lane on a motorway is the extra lane which allows you to slow down safely before entering the exit slip road. There, and in the ordinary road beyond, traffic conditions and speed will be quite different from those obtaining on the motorway. The deceleration or 'slowing down' lane is somewhat like the de-pressurisation chamber which deep sea divers have to enter in order to normalise before return to surface pressure above.* (Rules 185 & 186)

27. *You must leave the motorway at the next exit.* (Page 54)

28. *When normal conditions prevail on the motorway, the special signs are completely blank.* (Rule 171)

29. *Flashing amber signals indicate danger in some form. This might be an obstruction due to an accident, slippery road surfaces ahead which could cause skidding, or perhaps a patch of fog of which you are unaware.* (Rule 171)

30. *FALSE! NEVER EVER retrieve a fallen object from the motorway yourself. Instead, leave it and watch out for the nearest roadside telephone, from which you can telephone and inform the police of what has happened and where it has occurred.* (Rule 178)

ANSWERS: THE ROAD

31. Briefly on a motorway or unrestricted dual carriageway, to warn drivers behind of a hazard ahead. Otherwise, you may only use them when stationary, as a warning that your car is obstructing traffic.
(Rule 134)

32. a) At least 50 metres from your car.
b) At least 150 metres from your car. (Rule 150)

33. They should wear: tough clothing (for protection in case they fall off); reflective/fluorescent clothes; eye protection. They should use dipped headlights to help visibility. (Rule 30)

34. Take a basic training course. (Rule 37)

35. Traffic signs that give orders. (Rule 44)

36. Mirror. Signal. Look round. Only move when safe.
(Rule 48)

37. 30 mph. (Rule 54)

38. 20 mph. (Rule 55)

39. When wet, icy or foggy, or at night. (Rule 56)

40. Check for obstructions and pedestrians behind the car (especially children). You should be aware of the blind spot where you cannot see the road.
(Rule 129)

PASS YOUR HIGHWAY CODE TEST

Section Two: Other Road Users

41. Motor vehicles over 7,500 kg maximum gross weight and trailers over 3,500 kg maximum gross weight.
(Page 56)

42. Rectangular boards painted in red and yellow slanted stripes. (Page 66)

43. Having wound down the driver's window, extend your arm and make an anticlockwise circular movement with it. (Page 57)

44. You extend your arm from the driver's window and move it up and down. (Page 57)

45. a) Indicates the point at which you should give way to traffic from the right at a 'mini' roundabout.
    b) Indicates the point where you must give way to traffic on a major road.
    c) Indicates the point at which you should give way to traffic from the right on a roundabout.
(Page 63)

46. The sign shows a single-decker bus with a direction arrow and the words BUS LANE. (Page 62)

47. The other feature is the rear end of a car towing the caravan. (Page 62)

48. A rectangular panel with a light blue background and a pedal cycle illustrated in white. (Page 62)

ANSWERS: OTHER ROAD USERS

49. You should make a habit of glancing in your rear-view mirrors regularly in order to see who is behind you and what they are doing. Use them well before you carry out any manoeuvre. (Rule 51)

50. Leave a 2 second gap. (Rule 57)

51. Ambulances. Fire engines. Police vehicles. (Rule 76)

52. a) Yes.
    b) No.
    c) No.
    d) Yes.
    e) No. (Road traffic law C)

53. To move back into the left-hand lane as soon as possible without cutting in. (Rule 169)

54. In all cases, an emergency vehicle is approaching. (Rule 76)

55. The led horse should be on the left, with the rider between it and the traffic. (Rule 220)

56. At left hand bends and on narrow country roads, herds of animals cannot be seen in advance by oncoming drivers. Drive past slowly, giving them plenty of room. Don't rev your engine or sound your horn. (Rule 80)

57. a) No.
    b) No.
    c) No.
    d) Yes.
    e) No. (Rule 155)

PASS YOUR HIGHWAY CODE TEST

58. No. It is an offence to pick up hitchhikers on motorways, including slip roads. (Rule 181)

59. A herd of animals being driven, or people marching. (Rules 5 & 215)

60. Check that pedestrians, cyclists and other vehicles on the road are not so near that they will collide with your open door. (Rule 137)

61. a) NO. Use full headlights.
    b) NO. Use side lights only.
    c) YES.
    d) YES. (Rule 132)

62. If you wish another road user to be aware of your presence. (Rule 135)

63. If you wish to warn other road users of your presence. (Rule 136)

64. NO. You should wait until it actually turns left before you drive on. Never ASSUME the signal is correct. Wait and make sure first. (Rule 111)

65. On its right. (Rule 102)

66. Pedestrians on the pavement. (Rule 69)

67. When someone has stepped onto the crossing. (Rule 71)

ANSWERS: OTHER ROAD USERS

68. When pedestrians want to cross the road you should not signal them to cross because, although you may be willing to stop for them, you cannot know whether other approaching vehicles will do the same.
(Rule 71)

69. A pedestrian crossing. Don't park or overtake in the marked area. (Rule 72)

70. Keep pedestrian crossings clear. (Rule 73)

71. When a straight Pelican crossing has a central refuge it is *ONE* crossing, but with a staggered crossing (i.e. not in a straight line), it is operated as *TWO* separate crossings. (Rules 15 & 74)

72. *STOP . . . CHILDREN.* (Rule 66 & Page 58)

sign 1q

73. The location of the accident and details of any casualties. (Rule 153)

74. NO. Stop if you see the barrier descending or the level crossing gates starting to close, or if red or amber lights show. (Rule 226)

75. Holidaymakers, probably with cars loaded with luggage. HR means 'Holiday Route'. (Page 62)

PASS YOUR HIGHWAY CODE TEST

76. a) *Skull and crossbones. White.*
    b) *Flames. White above and red below.*
    c) *Gas cylinder. Green.*
    d) *Three triangles around a black dot. White.*
    e) *Test tubes pouring drops onto a bar and a hand. Black below and white above.*
    f) *Flames on a black circle. Yellow.*
    g) *Flames. Red.* (Page 66)

77. *A triangle with white and red slanted stripes.* (Page 66)

78. *Watch for them. Take appropriate action.* (Rule 46)

79. *When entering or leaving property.* (Rule 50)

80. *Flashing amber.* (Rule 77)

81. *Horse riders are often children.* (Rule 81)

82. a) *Only if it's unavoidable.*
    b) *NO.* (Rule 98)

83. *Only overtake if safe. Make sure the road is clear. Don't get too close to the vehicle you are overtaking. Mirror. Signal. Take extra care in bad visibility.* (Rule 99)

84. *Pass quickly, leaving lots of room. Move back to the left as soon as you can without cutting in.* (Rule 100)

85. *As much room as a car.* (Rule 101)

ANSWERS: OTHER ROAD USERS

86. When the traffic in front is signalling right. In slow traffic queues, when the queue on your right is slower (but don't move to the left except to turn left).
(Rules 102 & 103)

87. Don't speed up. You may slow down to help the overtaking car. (Rule 104)

88. Don't overtake where you can't see properly, such as: on a corner or bend; on a hump bridge; on the brow of a hill. Also don't overtake where you would conflict with others, such as: approaching a junction; where the road is narrow; near a school crossing patrol; where you would drive over chevrons; where you would enter a bus or cycle lane; between a tram and the kerb at a tram stop; where cars are waiting in a queue; at a level crossing; or where you would make someone slow or swerve. (Rule 106)

Section Three:
Driving Conditions and Night Driving

89. The word FORD. (Page 60)

90. a) No.
    b) Yes.
    c) No.
    d) Yes.
    e) Yes, but not during prohibited times.
    f) No, except to pick up or set down passengers.
(Rules 138 & 142)

91. Between 11.30 p.m. and 7.00 a.m. (Rule 136)

PASS YOUR HIGHWAY CODE TEST

92. 60 miles per hour. (Rule 57)

93. At least doubled, but this is a minimum. The greater distance between yourself and the car in front commensurate with other road safety factors, the better. (Rule 57)

94. Outside its period of operation. However, some bus lanes are in operation for the whole 24 hours and so may never be used by other vehicles. (Rule 97)

95. In conditions of fog or mist or at night or dusk it can be more difficult to judge speed and distance than it is during the daytime. (Rule 99)

96. No. (Rule 103)

97. You should watch out for pedestrians crossing the road into which you are turning. You must be prepared to give way to them. (Rule 108)

98. They stay blank and without flashing lights. (Rule 171)

99. The amber lights flash. (Rule 171)

100. That there is a sharp bend to the left ahead. (Page 59)

101. An exclamation mark means that there is a danger unspecified by another sign lying ahead. There may, for example, be a flood in the road due to a blocked drain, or a tree could have fallen across the road.

ANSWERS: DRIVING CONDITIONS

Sometimes the sign with the exclamation mark may be accompanied by another sign detailing the danger in words. (Page 60)

102. *Two pairs of alternating flashing red lights, and maybe a red cross.* (Rule 172)

103. *Keep on driving!* (Rule 226)

104. *Wait at the side until both halves of the dual carriageway are clear enough for you to turn into it in one continuous movement.* (Rule 112)

105. *Avoid doing anything that will frighten the animals, such as driving by too fast, sounding your horn or 'revving' your engine.* (Rule 80)

106. *It is a hazard warning sign.* (Rule 83)

107. *By telephoning the signalman, using the special railway telephone provided. If it is safe to cross, do so as quickly as possible, then telephone the signalman again to advise that you have done so.* (Rule 229)

108. *By looking both ways and listening.* (Rule 234)

109. *10 metres (32 feet).* (Rule 143)

110. *Standing behind the rear of your vehicle when it has broken down at night could obscure the rear lamps.* (Rule 150)

111. *Another train is approaching.* (Rule 227)

PASS YOUR HIGHWAY CODE TEST

112. *Facing in the direction of traffic flow.* (Rule 142)

113. *Give the emergency services details of the labels and markings on the side of the vehicle. These indicate the nature of the dangerous contents.* (Rule 154)

114. *The pedestrian is both deaf and blind.* (Rule 64)

115. *They may not be able to judge speeds well and, in misjudging the speed of your oncoming car, could step out into the road unexpectedly.* (Rule 64)

116. *The short red bar across a line indicating a route shows that the route is closed.* (Page 62)

117. *Because other road users could be endangered by seeing you too late.* (Rule 140)

118. *a) Yes.*
     b) Yes.
     c) Yes. Headlamps must be used where the street lights are more than 185 metres (600 feet) apart.
     d) No. Seriously reduced visibility is reckoned at less than 100 metres (328 feet). (Rule 131)

119. *You should not wear tinted spectacles at night nor in conditions of poor visibility, since they restrict your vision and this could be dangerous.* (Rule 35)

120. *The first sign indicates that the road narrows on the right only. The second sign shows that it narrows on both sides.* (Page 59)

ANSWERS: DRIVING CONDITIONS

121. *A triangular red-edged sign showing a deer in silhouette.*

    sign 5k

122. *Only drive if your journey is essential. Make sure your windows and lights are clean and working. Use dipped headlights, or fog lights if visibility is severely reduced. Use wipers and demisters. Slow down. Leave a safe gap to the car in front. Don't hang on to the tail lights of the car in front. Watch your speed (you may be going faster than you think). Use your brakes if you slow down. Don't speed up to get away from the car behind. Be careful of patchy fog, which you can run into suddenly.* (Rule 58)

123. *Put anti-freeze in the radiator, and keep the battery well maintained.* (Rule 59)

124. *Take care when passing a gritting lorry, especially if you are a motorcyclist.* (Rule 60)

125. *Keep in the highest gear you can.* (Rule 61)

126. *When the snow has been cleared from the lane you want to use.* (Rule 62)

127. *Watch out for any road signs and act on them, including ones showing a temporary speed limit.* (Rules 147 & 148)

PASS YOUR HIGHWAY CODE TEST

Section Four: Motorways, Primary Routes and Local Roads

128. The sign shows a two-lane road with a bridge over it in white. (Page 62)

sign 6a

129. Motorway signs have light blue backgrounds. Primary route signs have green backgrounds. The most common local road signs have white backgrounds. (Page 61)

130. Drive at a steady speed that you and your car can both cope with. Don't exceed the limit for your type of vehicle. Leave a safe gap to the vehicle in front. Increase the gap on slippery roads. (Rule 161)

131. It means that the M1 can be reached from the M10 at a point further along the M10. (Page 61)

132. a) FALSE, except when traffic is moving slowly in queues and the queue on your right is slower.
     b) FALSE. (Rule 167)

133. You will normally approach from a slip road on the left. Give way to traffic on the motorway. Look for a safe gap. Join the left hand lane at the same speed as traffic in that lane. Where the slip road continues as

ANSWERS: MOTORWAYS AND PRIMARY ROADS

a lane on the motorway, stay in that lane. After joining, don't overtake until you are used to the speed of the traffic.   (Rules 158, 159 & 160)

134. a) Red.
b) Amber.
c) Green.   (Rule 174)

135. One or more lanes may be closed. The speed limit may be lower than normal.   (Rule 177)

136. No.   (Rule 163)

137. a) TRUE.
b) TRUE.   (Rule 164)

138. Only overtake if you're sure it's safe. Make sure the lane you are joining is clear (traffic may come up fast from behind). Mirror. Signal. Take extra care in poor visibility.   (Rule 168)

139. On the hard shoulder.   (Rule 183)

140. On the left-hand side.   (Rule 185)

141. A lighted arrow bent to the left.   (Page 54)

142. Because speeds can seem slower than they really are. For example: 50 mph can seem like 30 mph.
   (Rule 186)

143. First, look to see if there is a telephone immediately in sight. If not, look at the arrows on the posts at the back of the hard shoulder which show you the direction of the nearest telephone.   (Rule 183)

PASS YOUR HIGHWAY CODE TEST

144. *Each white bar represents 100 yards.* (Page 62)

145. *That you should change lanes.* (Page 54)

146. *Before you take your vehicle on the motorway, make sure it's fit; check fuel, oil, water and tyre pressures, and make sure windows, lights, reflectors and mirrors are clean. On the motorway use your mirrors early and look further ahead than you would on normal roads.* (Rules 156 & 157)

147. *Short, white, widely-spaced bars.* (Page 63)

148. *You DON'T move it. You extend your arm and hold it there.* (Page 57)

149. *That you are slowing down or intend to stop.* (Page 57)

150. *You are telling the police officer that you want to drive straight on.* (Page 57)

151. *He is telling the traffic in front of him to STOP!* (Page 55)

152. *Go if you can clear the junction, or are taking up position to turn right.* (Rule 114)

153. *To your right. Your car and the other car should be offside to offside unless the layout of the junction makes this impractical, or nearside to nearside passing is indicated, either by road markings or the position of the other vehicle.* (Rules 118 & 119)

ANSWERS: MOTORWAYS AND PRIMARY ROADS

154. *In the gap in the central reservation.* (Rule 120)

155. *a) No.*
     b) Yes, if you can do so safely.
     c) Yes.
     d) Yes. (Rules 102 & 103)

156. *The green GO signal will shortly follow the red/amber signal, but don't start until it does.*
     (Rule 114 & Page 54)

157. *They are both GIVE WAY signs. The eight-sided sign means you must STOP and GIVE WAY. The triangular sign means GIVE WAY TO TRAFFIC ON MAJOR ROAD AHEAD.*
     (Rule 109 & Page 58)

158. *Signal right as you approach the roundabout. Change to left signal after you pass the SECOND exit (the one before yours).* (Rule 124)

159. *Definitely not!* (Rule 130)

160. *To help or warn other road users. Give them clearly and in plenty of time. Make sure they cancel afterwards.* (Rule 45)

161. *Pull in at the first opportunity (possibly at a passing place or layby) and allow the faster vehicle to overtake.* (Rule 104)

162. *When there is a serious reduction in visibility i.e. to less than 100 metres (328 feet).* (Rule 133)

PASS YOUR HIGHWAY CODE TEST

163. *When one is available.* (Rule 40)

164. *The extra, crawler, lane on some hills is to be used by slow moving vehicles.* (Rule 88)

165. *Hazard. Don't cross the line unless you can see the road is clear for a long way.* (Rule 83)

166. *Stop opposite the passing place so that the oncoming vehicle may use it.* (Rule 82)

167. *Vehicles in the main road have the right of way.* (Rule 110)

168. *For overtaking or for turning right.* (Rule 95)

169. *When there are slower vehicles in the left-hand lane. However, once you have passed them, you should return to the left-hand lane.* (Rule 95)

170. *By moving, in good time, to the correct lane for your exit. This will be the right hand lane unless signs or markings say otherwise.* (Rule 96)

171. *a) No.*
     b) Yes.
     c) No.
     d) Yes. (Rule 89)

172. *a) Middle lane.*
     b) Middle lane. (Rule 92)

173. *Pull in when safe so that other people can get past you.* (Rule 53)

ANSWERS: MOTORWAYS AND PRIMARY ROADS

174. *They will flash their headlights or blue light, sound their horn or siren, and direct you to the side of the road by using their indicators and pointing.*
(Rule 78)

175. *You should not try to jump the queue by changing lanes.* (Rule 91)

176. *The lanes on the right hand side.* (Rule 93)

177. *For turning right or overtaking.* (Rule 94)

Section Five: You and Your Car

178. *At the age of fourteen.* (Rule 40)

179. *Well-behaved or not, you should never let your dog out of your car without first attaching a lead.*
(Rule 213)

180. *Behind the rear seats.* (Rule 42)

181. *Cover or remove the L-plates.* (Rule 38)

182. *The driver and front-seat passenger, and any rear-seat passengers in vehicles where belts are fitted on rear seats, unless exempt.* (Rule 40)

183. *That it is suitable for the child's age and weight (or size).* (Rule 41)

184. *The use of child safety locks, where fitted.* (Rule 42)

PASS YOUR HIGHWAY CODE TEST

185. *By flashing your lights or sounding your car horn.* (Rules 135 & 136)

186. *When you are feeling tired or are unwell, even if it's only a slight cold.* (Rule 31)

187. *Improperly adjusted headlamps can dazzle other road users and cause an accident.* (Rule 131)

188. *By showing him the palm of your upraised left hand.* (Page 57)

189. *Have a break. Pull in at the first suitable parking place or layby and rest for a while until you feel more refreshed. Make sure there is plenty of fresh air in the car.* (Rule 32)

190. *You have forgotten to make the appropriate signal i.e. use your direction indicator.* (Rule 117)

191. *Lock it.* (Rule 137)

192. *Tyres, exhaust system and windscreen wipers.* (Rule 28)

193. *Check to make sure you won't hit or obstruct others (look particularly for bikes).* (Rule 137)

194. *No.* (Rule 134)

195. *You did not place the reflecting triangle far enough away from your car. On an ordinary road, a distance of 50 metres is sufficient. On the motorway, this should be trebled, to 150 metres.* (Rule 150)

ANSWERS: YOU AND YOUR CAR

196. *Windscreen wipers. Headlamps or front fog lamps.* (Rule 58)

197. *a) Your doctor.*
     b) The pharmacist. (Rule 33)

198. *20.5 metres (67 feet).* (Rule 34)

199. *In bad visibility, or at night.* (Rule 35)

200. *You must be over 21, and have had a licence for that type of car for at least 3 years.* (Rule 36)

201. *It reduces coordination. It affects your judgement of speed, distance and risk. It slows down your reactions. It gives you false confidence.* (Rule 39)

202. *Only when it has a hands-free microphone AND it will not take your mind off the road. Don't use a hand-held phone/microphone.* (Rule 43)

Section Six: Markings on the Road

203. *A rectangular space enclosed in broken white lines with BUS STOP written inside.* (Page 65)

204. *By white arrows painted on the road surface. Also, in some cases, place names or road numbers painted on the surface.* (Page 65)

205. *The entrance to a side road.* (Page 65)

PASS YOUR HIGHWAY CODE TEST

206. SCHOOL. Entrance to be kept clear of stationary vehicles, even if picking up or setting down children. (Page 65)

207. A 'mini' roundabout. (Page 63)

208. The stop line at the STOP sign is broader. (Page 63)

209. a) Three yellow lines.
     b) One line.
     c) Two lines. (Rule 145 & Page 64)

210. Short, white, widely-spaced bars. (Rule 87 & Page 63)

211. A double broken white line across the road and sometimes an inverted white triangle on the road surface just before the junction. (Pages 63 & 65)

212. Yellow lines painted ON THE ROAD indicate waiting restrictions. Yellow lines painted ON THE KERB indicate loading and unloading restrictions. (Page 64)

213. The double yellow line. (Page 64)

214. Long, white rectangles, spaced their own length apart. (Page 63)

215. A point at which you must give way to other traffic. (Page 65)

216. a) Yes.
     b) No.
     c) Yes. (Rule 86 & Page 63)

ANSWERS: MARKINGS ON THE ROAD

217. a) No.
 b) Yes.
 c) Yes.
 d) No. (Rule 84)

218. You may cross the broken white line when overtaking as long as it is safe to do so. In addition, you must be able to complete your overtaking, that is return safely to the left hand driving lane, BEFORE the start of double white lines on the road which have the solid line nearer to you. (Rule 85)

219. Zigzag lines on either side of the driving lane. (Page 65)

220. a) Amber studs indicate the central reservation of dual carriageways.
 b) Red studs mark the edge of the carriageway on the left-hand side.
 c) White studs are often used in conjuction with white lines to indicate the centre of a road, or to mark road lanes.
 d) Green studs are used to indicate laybys and side roads. (Rule 87)

221. Definitely not. (Rules 72 & 106)

222. In theory, yes. Until a pedestrian puts a foot on the crossing you are not obliged to stop, BUT you should give precedence to pedestrians who are waiting to cross. (Rule 71)

223. Green studs on a motorway indicate the line separating the slip-roads from the through carriageway. (Rule 174)

PASS YOUR HIGHWAY CODE TEST

224. *Red studs on a motorway indicate the left-hand edge of the carriageway.* (Rule 174)

225. *Yes, but only in an emergency, such as a manoeuvre that will avoid an accident.* (Rule 86 & Page 63)

226. *Don't enter the marked area unless your exit road is clear, though you can enter if you want to turn right and your way is blocked by oncoming or right turning traffic.* (Rule 113 & Page 65)

Section Seven: Signs on the Road

227. *Triangular.* (Page 59)

228. *No pedestrians.* (Page 58)

229. *The arrows, one above the other, point right (top) and left (bottom).* (Page 59)

sign 3d

230. *The light signals have failed.* (Page 59)

231. *No overtaking. The sign implies that the red car — red because it is in a dangerous position in a 'no overtaking' situation — is the overtaking car.*
(Page 58)

ANSWERS: SIGNS ON THE ROAD

232. A diamond-shaped sign, white at the top and red at the bottom. The white part shows black and white 'flames' and the lower part, the words SPONTANEOUSLY COMBUSTIBLE. 'Spontaneously combustible' means that the material is volatile and can burst into flames or burn on its own. (Page 66)

233. a) is carried on the side of the vehicle.
 b) at the rear. (Page 66)

234. At airfields, lifting bridges, level crossings or fire stations. (Page 54)

235. These signs give orders and are mostly prohibitive. (Page 58)

236. The sign indicates a segregated pedal cyclist and pedestrian route. (Page 59)

237. The first sign means that 30 mph is the minimum speed. The second indicates that this speed limit no longer applies. (Page 59)

238. a) Two arrows pointing to the bottom right and left of the circle mean that vehicles may pass on either side.
 b) Three arrows round the edge of a blue circular sign are found at 'mini' roundabouts. This means, by inference, that you must give way to vehicles coming from the immediate right.
 (Page 59)

signs 2t, 2z

PASS YOUR HIGHWAY CODE TEST

239. The sign with the gate indicates a level crossing with a barrier or gate. The sign with the steam engine indicates that the level crossing ahead has NO barrier or gate. (Page 60)

240. The sign indicates low flying aircraft in the vicinity or that there may be sudden aircraft noise which could startle you. The sign is a white, red-edged, upright triangle. (Page 60)

sign 3u

241. The signs are white with black borders and black printing. (Page 61)

242. A green, yellow-edged sign showing the letter 'R'. (Page 61)

243. The sign indicates a diversion route. (Page 62)

244. The arrows tell you to GET IN LANE for the destinations shown on another, blue, panel above the black one. (Page 61)

sign 6g

245. No. The sign means that no motor vehicles apart from solo motorcycles, scooters and mopeds are allowed to use the road. (Page 58)

ANSWERS: SIGNS ON THE ROAD

246. An exclamation mark in black is shown on a triangular, white, red-edged sign. (Page 60)

247. That there are wild animals in the vicinity. There are, however, other signs indicating the presence of specific wild animals, such as badgers or frogs and toads. (Page 60)

248. The sign is in two parts. The larger, upper part contains a light blue circle edged in red, with a red diagonal and the words METER ZONE beneath. The lower, smaller panel indicates the periods at which the meters can be used. (Page 62)

249. Children may be crossing. (Rule 65 & Page 60)

250. Two green, downward-pointing arrows above the lanes which are open. Two red 'X's above the lanes which are closed. The use of red, of course, implies danger if you were unwise enough to try to proceed along the 'closed' lanes. (Page 54)

251. The sign is a white rectangle which shows, in black, the rear end of a car towing a caravan. (Page 62)

252. The sign indicates a hospital nearby. The word 'hospital' is, in fact, written under the 'H' on the sign. (Page 62)

253. 200 yards. (Page 62)

254. The sign denotes NO THROUGH ROAD.
(Page 62)

PASS YOUR HIGHWAY CODE TEST

255. *A panel with alternating flashing amber lights. In the centre panel, the left and the centre lanes are shown as straight vertical lines. The right-hand lane, however, shows as a vertical line with two horizontal bars across the top. All the lanes on this sign are indicated by means of lines of lights.* (Page 54)

256. *The word End spelled out in lights.* (Page 54)

257. *Do not proceed further in this lane.* (Page 54)

258. *The approach of a train, soon to arrive on the level crossing.* (Rule 226 & Page 54)

259. *PERMIT HOLDERS ONLY, meaning that parking is restricted to those holding permits to park there, for instance, residents.* (Page 58)

260. *The long, black, horizontal sign will show a line of white chevrons pointing to the left.* (Page 59)

261. *A red edged diagonal cross.* (Page 60)

sign 4k

262. *A white, red-edged triangle with a broken black circle in the centre.* (Page 59)

sign 5b

ANSWERS: SIGNS ON THE ROAD

263. *Signs showing silhouettes of people could feature two elderly folk; an adult and a child, showing that there are pedestrians on the road ahead; a man walking, indicating a pedestrian crossing ahead; two children running, showing the presence nearby of a school; a man digging, indicating road works.* (Page 60)

just triangular parts of signs 4j, 4h, 5i, 4l

264. *That the road ahead is about to narrow on both sides.* (Page 59)

265. *The round blue sign which has a smaller arrow means AHEAD ONLY. The rectangular blue sign, which has a larger arrow, means ONE-WAY TRAFFIC.* (Page 59)

Section Eight: Roundabouts and Level Crossings

266. *They may keep to the left. They may also indicate right to show they are staying on the roundabout.* (Rule 126)

267. *Vehicles making U-turns, and long vehicles which may have to cross the centre of the roundabout.* (Rule 128)

268. *Use the normal roundabout rules at each one.* (Rule 123)

PASS YOUR HIGHWAY CODE TEST

269. *Traffic coming from your right.* (Rule 123)

270. *On reaching a roundabout, decide which exit you want and get in lane.* (Rule 123)

271. *Approach in the left-hand lane, signalling left. Keep doing this through the roundabout.* (Rule 124)

272. *They may have to take a different course. Watch for their signals and leave them lots of room.* (Rule 127)

273. *Approach in the right-hand lane and keep to it. Signal right on approach, and change to left as you pass the exit before yours.* (Rule 124)

274. *a) When turning left or going straight on.*
 b) When turning right or going full circle.
(Rule 124)

275. *Stop.* (Rule 231)

276. *No. The flashing STOP lights indicate that a second train is approaching the level crossing.* (Rule 227)

277. *Never drive onto the crossing unless the exit is clear. Don't stop on or just after it. Don't drive nose to tail over it.* (Rule 225)

278. *Never zigzag around the barriers.* (Rule 228)

279. *GIVE WAY. Always give way to trains.* (Rule 234)

280. *An audible alarm.* (Rule 226)

ANSWERS: ROUNDABOUTS

281. *Get passengers clear of the crossing. Phone the signal operator. Try to move the car, but get clear if the signals start showing a train is coming.*
(Rule 230)

282. *The half-barrier at an automatic level crossing has red and white vertical stripes.* (Page 49)

283. *A level crossing without barrier or gate.* (Page 60)

284. *Diamond shaped.* (Rule 235)

285. *Stop. Look both ways. Open gates both sides. Check for trains again. Cross quickly. Close gates. Phone signal operator before and after, if there is a telephone.* (Rule 233)

286. *A white, red-edged triangle with a broken black circle in the centre.* (Page 59)

287. *A level crossing with barrier or gate.* (Page 60)

288. *A white diagonal cross with red edges.* (Page 60)

289. *The sign for Trams Crossing Ahead is a red edged triangle with a black tram in it.* (Page 60)

290. *NO. You MUST NOT enter a lane reserved for trams.* (Rule 235)

291. *a) No.*
b) Definitely not.
c) Yes, driving on is the right thing to do and as quickly as safety will allow. (Rule 226)

292. *The most appropriate lane.* (Rule 124)

293. *The lane which follows through from the lane by which you originally approached the roundabout.* (Rule 124)

294. *Don't signal on approach. Approach in left or centre lane, or right if left is blocked. Keep to same lane through roundabout. Signal left after passing exit before your one.* (Rule 124)

295. *You signal a left on the approach.* (Rule 124)

296. *Normally, the lane in which you approach the roundabout depends on whether you wish to turn right or left or to go forward when leaving the roundabout. Approach in the left-hand lane when turning left or going forward; approach in the right-hand lane when turning right.* (Rule 124)

297. *When turning right at a roundabout, signal with your right-hand indicator. Keep the indicator operating until you reach the exit before the one you wish to take. Then change to the left-hand indicator.* (Rule 124)

298. *First an amber light, and then flashing red lights.* (Rule 226)

299. *Look up the track and down the track to check whether you can see a train on the line. Looking both ways like this, as well as listening for the sound of an approaching train should needless to say be done from the edge of the railway line.* (Rule 234)

ANSWERS: ROUNDABOUTS

300. *You must not park where you would get in the way of trams.* (Rule 239)

301. *Drivers of large and/or slow-moving vehicles must telephone the line signalman, using the special railway telephone provided. Being able to view the state of the track further away from the level crossing, the signalman can tell the driver if it is safe to cross. Once over the crossing, the driver must telephone back to the signalman to inform him of this fact.* (Rule 299)

302. *a) You MUST follow the route shown by signs and markings.*
 b) You MUST NOT drive between the left-hand kerb and the tram. (Rule 238)

303. *Where the track changes from one side of the road to the other, or gets close to the kerb.* (Rule 237)

304. *Don't cross on red. On green, open gates both sides. Check light is still green. Cross. Close gates.* (Rule 232)

305. *First of all, watch out for vehicles crossing or about to cross in front of your own, and give way to them.* (Rule 125)

PASS YOUR HIGHWAY CODE TEST

Section Nine: Waiting and Parking

306. NO. You should wait until the oncoming vehicle has passed before moving out a sufficient distance to the right in order to pass the parked vehicle.
(Rule 105)

307. The colour of a Disabled Person's badge is orange and people without it MUST NOT park in the reserved space. (Rule 141)

308. Watch out for pedestrians, especially children. Children are more interested in ice-cream than in passing cars. (Rules 63 & 67)

309. You are not allowed to park your car anywhere on the motorway, except in case of breakdown or accident, when you may park on the hard shoulder.
(Rules 138, 179 & 180)

310. No. You may never park at night against the traffic direction. (Rule 142)

311. An authorised parking space. (Rules 140 & 143)

312. No. (Rule 140)

313. Don't park where you would make other vehicles enter a tram lane. (Rule 140)

314. Near the brow of a hill or a hump bridge.
(Rule 140)

ANSWERS: WAITING AND PARKING

315. *The vehicle must not be left unattended.*   (Rule 146)

316. *Because parking opposite a traffic island would unduly narrow the road and restrict the movement of vehicles along the road.*   (Rule 140)

317. *You should leave your sidelights on.*   (Rule 144)

318. *You must check that the door will not hit cyclists, pedestrians, or any road users close behind or make them swerve.*   (Rule 137)

319. *. . . if it would cause an obstruction.*   (Rule 140)

320. *You must pull up your handbrake firmly.*
(Rule 137)

321. *30 mph or less.*   (Rule 143)

322. *10 metres.*   (Rules 140 & 143)

323. *To set down or pick up passengers.*   (Rule 138)

324. *a) No.*
b) No. You can never park on a clearway.
c) Yes, but only then.
d) No.   (Rule 138)

325. *a) FALSE.*
b) TRUE.
c) FALSE.   (Rules 140 & 143)

326. *You must always have your dog on a lead when on or near a road and that applies whether it is well-behaved or not.*   (Rule 212)

327. *AT ANY TIME.* (Page 64)

328. *Plates with light blue backgrounds.* (Page 64)

329. *Yellow lines over the kerb indicate restrictions on loading and unloading.* (Rule 145)

330. *Along the edge of the road.* (Rule 139)

331. *Loading restrictions during every working day and other times.* (Page 64)

332. *Periods other than every working day.* (Page 64)

333. *Red lines.* (Rule 139)

334. *Most definitely FALSE!* (Rule 180)

335. *Just as definitely FALSE!* (Rule 180)

336. *You can find out when you are not allowed to park from signs at the kerb or at the entrance to the controlled parking zone.* (Rule 139)

337. *Lights.* (Rule 143)

338. *Whenever possible.* (Rule 137)

339. *No.* (Rule 225)

340. *No. A pavement is for pedestrians and not vehicles, no matter how wide it may be.* (Rule 140)

ANSWERS: WAITING AND PARKING

341. a) No.
     b) No.
     c) Yes.
     d) No. (Rule 140)

342. On the side by the kerb. (Rule 137)

343. Leave plenty of room. (Rule 137)

344. As near to the kerb as possible. (Rule 137)

345. No. (Rule 82)

Section Ten: Breakdowns, Accidents and Mishaps

346. Think of others and get your car off the road if you can. (Rule 149)

347. Warn other traffic. Switch off engines. Don't let anyone smoke. Call the emergency services. Don't move the injured unless they are in danger. Give first aid if needed. Move uninjured away. Stay at the scene until emergency services arrive. (Rule 153)

348. a) 150 metres (492 feet).
     b) 50 metres (164 feet). (Rule 150)

349. Warning signs, the flashing lights of emergency vehicles, and traffic in the distance moving slowly or stopped. (Rule 152)

350. You should not stand at the rear of your car because other drivers may not see your rear lights and will be unaware of your presence. (Rule 150)

351. The location of the accident, and details of casualties. (Rule 153)

352. No. You should never remove a motorcyclist's helmet unless absolutely necessary. (Rule 153)

353. a) Orange reflectorised plates.
b) Diamond-shaped hazard warning plates.
(Rule 154)

354. Keep uninjured where the wind won't blow substances towards them. Don't risk yourself, even to save life. Tell emergency services about labels.
(Rule 154)

355. Dangerous liquids spilled on the roadway may give off vapours or may contaminate dust lying on the road. While it is always advisable to keep well away from the vehicle concerned, the wind may carry vapours or dust towards you. It is therefore wise to test the direction of the wind in order to know where to position yourself more safely. (Rule 154)

356. Pull into a service area if you can. If not then pull onto the hard shoulder, as far to the left as possible. (Rule 183)

ANSWERS: BREAKDOWNS

357. Yes, the driver in this question has done the right thing. The alternative — stopping his car and getting out to retrieve the paddle — would be far more dangerous both to himself and other traffic. It is, in any case, banned in the Highway Code. The driver is also correct in pulling over onto the hard shoulder, which can be used in emergency, and telephoning the police. (Rule 178)

358. As soon as it's safe to do so, stop and retrieve it. (Rule 151)

359. No. If you're distracted you may cause another accident. (Rule 152)

360. a) By doors on the left-hand side of the car.
     b) Near the vehicle but away from the carriageway or hard shoulder. (Rule 183)

361. Follow the arrows on the posts at the back of the hard shoulder. Don't cross the motorway. (Rule 183)

362. Use hazard warning lights. Only leave your vehicle if you can safely get off the carriageway. Otherwise, remain in the car with seat belt on. Don't put a warning triangle on the carriageway. (Rule 183)

363. Stay in the locked car. Use hazard warning lights. Display a 'Help' pennant. (Rule 183)

364. Build up speed on the hard shoulder. Look for a gap in traffic. (Rule 184

Section Eleven: First Aid on the Road

365. The second threatened danger is FIRE, perhaps from spilled petrol or other inflammable liquid or from a fractured petrol tank.

366. The location of the accident.

367. Apart from the inadvisability of smoking in the presence of injured people, there is the fire hazard mentioned in the answer to Question 365 above.

368. It is most definitely NOT wise. Accident victims should never be given anything to drink. They may have internal injuries which might worsen if they drink.

369. However hard it may be to refuse, casualties should not be moved unless there is the threat of danger from further collisions or from fire. Accident victims with back injuries may become paralysed if inexpertly moved and further damage could be inflicted to broken limbs.

370. Clear the mouth of obvious obstructions, such as false teeth.

371. Backwards, that is, as far back as possible. This is done in order to clear the victim's airway.

372. Apart from the comfort which the presence of another person may give to accident victims, they should not be left alone in case their condition sud-

ANSWERS: FIRST AID ON THE ROAD

denly gets worse, e.g. they stop breathing and become unconscious. The person who is with them can then give mouth-to-mouth resuscitation and may thereby save their lives. Accident victims should not be allowed to get cold because this will increase their discomfort and may also make their condition deteriorate.

373. Pinch the casualty's nostrils together so that the air blown into the mouth will reach the lungs.

374. When the victim's chest starts to rise.

375. A clean pad of material applied to the wound with firm hand pressure. Take care, though, not to press on foreign bodies in the wound, such as splinters of glass or pieces of metal, as this will make the wound worse and cause the victim extra pain.

376. Four seconds.

Section Twelve:
Road Junctions and Traffic Lights

377. At a junction you should give way to pedestrians crossing the road that you want to turn into.
(Rule 68)

378. While pedestrians are still crossing the road in front of you. (Rule 75)

379. *Get into the correct lane early. Be careful because some lanes lead directly off to another destination, so if you get the lane wrong you end up in the wrong place.* (Rules 165 & 175)

380. *No. This is most dangerous.* (Rule 106)

381. *Double broken white lines in front of your car, and maybe a 'Give Way' sign or a triangle painted in the road. You MUST give way to traffic on the main road.* (Rule 110)

382. *They may go in different directions. Get in lane early.* (Rule 90)

383. *Criss-cross lines painted in yellow at a junction, forming a 'box' which you may not enter unless your exit from it is clear.* (Rule 113)

384. *FALSE.* (Rule 113)

385. *Mirror. Signal right. When safe, move to just left of the middle of the road (or to the specially marked area). Try to leave room for others to pass on your left. Wait for a safe gap. Watch for pedestrians, cyclists, and motorcyclists. Turn without cutting the corner.* (Rule 117)

386. *Stop at the stop line as long as you are not already across the line or pulling up would cause an accident.* (Page 54)

ANSWERS: ROAD JUNCTIONS

387. *It allows traffic to turn while traffic driving straight on has to halt. 'Filtering off' the turning traffic helps to stop roads from becoming jammed and makes them easier to use for straight-on traffic. Don't join that lane unless you want to turn in the direction of the arrow.* (Rule 115)

388. *You should stop. However, the green light will follow shortly, allowing you to drive on.* (Rule 114)

389. *Because you need a safe gap in the traffic from both directions.* (Rule 117)

390. *Mirror. Signal left. Don't overtake bikes or horses just before turning. Watch for vehicles (especially cyclists) coming up on your left. Keep close to the left when turning.* (Rule 121)

391. *The sign shows a set of red, amber and green traffic lights with a red bar diagonally across them. You should proceed with care.* (Rule 116)

sign 3x

392. *No, wait until the road is clear. If you are kept waiting until the lights turn red again, so be it!* (Rule 114)

393. *You should look out for pedestrians, cyclists and motorcyclists, because junctions are more dangerous*

for them. You should also look out for long vehicles, because they may need the whole width of the road to turn. (Rule 107)

394. *No. This is the sign for No Through Road.*
(Page 62)

395. *He is about to turn right.* (Rule 120)

396. *No. Red and Amber together mean STOP.*
(Rule 114)

397. *Give way to any vehicles in the lane, whichever way they're moving.* (Rule 122)

398. *If you are already across the STOP line when the amber light shows you may drive on, and you may also do so if to stop may cause an accident.*
(Page 54)

399. *Red on its own. Red and amber together. Amber alone, except in the circumstances mentioned in answer 398 above.* (Page 54)

400. *The double white line painted on the road at a junction means that you should stop there in order to give way to any traffic on the road running across. If the latter is clear, you may drive on. When a solid white line is painted in the same place, you MUST stop.* (Rule 109)

ANSWERS: THREE DRIVER'S TALES

Section Thirteen: Three Driver's Tales

A. David saw the other car overtaking him out of his LEFT eye. This means he was being overtaken on the LEFT. Overtaking in such circumstances should always be on the RIGHT. (Rule 167)

B. The driver cut in front of David after overtaking. The Highway Code specifically states that overtaking cars should not cut in front but should have enough room after overtaking to move safely and smoothly in front of the vehicle just overtaken. (Rule 169)

C. No. David was driving at 40 mph on a wet road. He should therefore have reckoned 2 metres for every mile per hour of speed and the distance should have been 80 metres. Even on a dry road a 30 metre distance from the car in front when driving at 40 mph is too little. In these circumstances, the safe distance would be 40 metres minimum.

D. David should definitely NOT overtake, no matter what the provocation he has suffered. He should, instead, glance in his rear-view mirror to see that it is safe, then slacken speed and so drop back to a distance of at least 80 metres from the 'rogue' vehicle in front.

E. Unlike David, Anne and the children omitted to fasten their seat belts before moving off. (Rule 40)

F. The red-edged, white triangular sign indicating Road Works and depicting a man with a shovel.

PASS YOUR HIGHWAY CODE TEST

G. *The zigzag lines were painted along the edges and the centre of the road.*

H. *The pedestrians were reluctant to cross because Anne gave the signal for a left turn, not the signal for stopping which she intended — this comprises moving the arm up and down.*

I. *David sounded the car horn at 11.27 p.m. The prohibition against sounding car horns in built-up areas begins at 11.30 p.m.* (Rule 139)

J. *Yes. Three lamps going out reduced visibility in the road and must have increased the distance between lamps at that point to more than 185 metres.*

K. *Even though he was driving at night, when there would have been few pedestrians about, David kept to his daytime habit of looking to see if there were people crossing the side road he was about to enter. He did the correct thing.* (Rule 108)

L. *Anne was sitting in the passenger seat which meant, of course, that 'her' side of the road was the left-hand, near-side. Allowing that the parked cars had the right to be parked where they were, all Anne had to do to notice the incorrect parking was to count how many of the ten cars had their fronts to her as David was driving along. The four correctly parked cars were parked facing in the direction of the traffic flow.* (Rule 142)

ANSWERS: THE THEORY TEST

Section Fifteen: The Theory Test

1. c
2. b
3. a
4. d
5. c
6. b
7. d
8. d
9. c
10. b
11. a, b
12. b
13. b
14. a, c
15. a
16. c
17. c
18. b
19. a, b
20. b
21. b

INDEX

Note: the index indicates where questions about the topics are. The answers are on pages 77-125.

accidents 15, 20, 52, 53, 54, 55-7
aircraft 39
alcohol 31, 33
animals 12, 16, 19, 22, 30, 40, 50
bends 13, 42
box junctions 58-9
braking distance 5-6
breakdowns 9, 20, 24, 25, 32, 44, 52, 53, 54, 55
buses 6, 11, 12, 17, 18, 33, 49, 60
car phones 33, 74
caravans 11, 41
children 21, 30, 40, 73-4, 75
coaches 12
crawler lanes 28
cyclists 6, 11, 13, 16, 38, 43, 49, 60
danger *see* warnings
dangerous goods 15, 20, 38, 53
direction signs 7, 23, 25, 33, 39, 58, 69-70
disabled people 47, 52, 55
dogs 30, 50
dual carriageways 19, 26, 28, 29, 60, 72
emergency vehicles 11, 12
estate cars 30, 73-4
eyesight 32
first aid 55-7
flooded roads 74
fog 5, 6, 18, 22, 28, 32, 48, 73, 76
fords 17

fuel consumption 75
give way signs 11, 27, 34, 60
glasses, tinted 21, 32
goods vehicles 10, 12, 48, 49
hand signals 10, 26, 31, 63
hatchbacks 30, 73-4
hazards *see* warnings
headlights 13-14, 21, 31
health 31, 32
heavy goods vehicles 10, 12, 48
horns 14, 17, 64
horse riders 12, 16, 43
information signs 71
jams 14, 18, 29
junctions 18, 58-60
  bus lanes 11
  give way/stop signs 11, 27, 28, 34, 60
  left turns 10, 14, 43, 59, 60
  motorways 23, 24, 25, 41
  overtaking 58
  parking 20, 48, 49
  right turns 10, 19, 26, 29, 31, 59, 74
  road markings 33
  traffic lights 26, 59, 60
keep clear signs 33
lanes
  changing 28-9
  dual carriageways 28
  junctions 58
  motorways 40, 75
  overtaking on left 18, 23, 26-7, 75-6
  road markings 25

INDEX

lanes (*continued*)
  roundabouts 43, 45–6, 47
  signals 7, 8, 19, 25, 41, 42
learners 9, 13, 30, 33
left turns 10, 14, 43, 59, 60
level crossings 15, 19, 20, 39, 42, 44–5, 46, 47, 48, 51
lights (cars) 9, 13–14, 16, 20, 21, 28, 31, 32, 49, 76
load carrying 7, 9, 15, 16, 20, 38, 51, 53, 54, 76
L-plates 30
medicines 31, 32
mirrors 11
motorcyclists 9, 13, 16, 43, 49, 53
motorways 23–5
  breakdowns 24, 25, 32, 54, 55
  deceleration lane 8
  direction signs 23, 25, 58, 70
  fallen loads 54
  headlights 13
  hitchhikers 13
  junctions 23, 24, 25, 41
  lane discipline 40, 75
  lane signs 8, 19, 41, 42
  load carrying on 9
  overtaking 12, 23, 24
  permitted vehicles 12–13
  reversing 24
  right-hand lane 12
  road condition signs 8, 9, 18, 41
  roadworks 24
  sleepiness 6
  speed 23, 25
  stopping on 8, 48, 51, 73
  studs 23–4, 36
  telephones 25, 54
  warning triangles 9, 32, 53
moving off 9

narrow roads 21, 27, 28, 52, 74
night driving 13, 18, 20, 21, 64
one-way streets 17, 28
order-giving signs 65–6
overtaking 14, 16–17, 18, 29, 72
  driver's tale 61–2
  junctions 58
  left side 16, 18, 23, 26–7, 75–6
  motorways 12, 23, 24
  narrow roads 27, 29
  road markings 35, 36
  snow ploughs 22
  stationary vehicles 47
parking 17, 47–52
  actions on leaving car 13, 31, 32, 49
  caravans 11, 41
  disabled people 47, 52
  in fog 48
  hazard lights 32
  hills and bridges 21
  junctions 20, 48, 49
  level crossings 48, 51
  lights 20, 49
  meter zones 40
  motorways 48, 51
  pavements 50, 51
  permit holders 42
  trams 46, 48
  yellow lines 34–5, 50
pavements 16, 50, 51, 76
pedestrian crossings 10, 14, 15, 17, 36, 40, 49, 58, 63
pedestrians 7, 13, 14, 20, 21, 38, 58, 76
Pelican crossings 15, 17
police 26, 29, 31
queues 14, 18, 29
reversing 10, 24, 27
right-hand driving 7

127

PASS YOUR HIGHWAY CODE TEST

right-hand turns 10, 19, 26, 29, 31, 43, 59, 74
ring roads 40
road markings 33–6
road signs 37–42, 65–71
roadworks 22, 24, 62–3
roundabouts 7, 27, 34, 42, 43, 45–6, 47
schools 15, 40, 48, 75
seat belts 28, 30
sleepiness 6, 31
slow vehicles 16, 20, 29, 46
snow, driving in 22
spectacles, tinted 21, 32
speed limits 10, 38–9, 72
stop signs 27, 34, 38, 44
stopping distance 5–6, 11, 18
studs, in roads 23–4, 36
telephones 25, 33, 54, 74

theory test 72–6
thinking distance 5, 6
tiredness 6, 31
traffic islands 48
traffic lights 8, 26, 27, 58, 59, 60
traffic signs 65–71
trailer loads 12, 76
trams 45, 46, 47, 48, 49, 60
urban clearways 49
vision 32
waiting *see* parking
warning lights 9, 16, 32
warning signs 37, 40, 53, 67–9
warning triangles 9, 32, 53
wet weather 6, 18
wild animals 22, 40
winter driving 22
Zebra crossings 10, 14, 17, 36, 63